How to Achieve

Outstanding
Writers

in the
Early Years Foundation Stage
and Key Stage 1

Brilliant
PUBLICATIONS

Rowena Woods

We hope you and your pupils enjoy using the ideas in this book. Brilliant Publications publishes many other books to help teachers. To find out more details on any of the titles listed below, please go to our website: **www.brilliantpublications.co.uk**.

Other books published by Brilliant Publications:
Brilliant Activities for Reading Comprehension (6 book series)
Brilliant Activities for Grammar and Punctuation (6 book series)
Brilliant Activities for Creative Writing (6 book series)
Getting to Grips with English Grammar (6 book series)
Boost Creative Writing (3 book series)
Cracking Creative Writing
Daily Sentence Structures
Boost Spelling Skills

Published by Brilliant Publications Limited
Unit 10
Sparrow Hall Farm
Edlesborough
Dunstable
Bedfordshire
LU6 2ES, UK

www.brilliantpublications.co.uk

The name Brilliant Publications and the logo are registered trademarks.

Written by Rowena Woods
© Brilliant Publications Limited 2021

Printed ISBN: 978-0-85747-838-2

The book and USB Drive cannot be sold separately.

First printed and published in the UK in 2021
10 9 8 7 6 5 4 3 2 1

Contents

All photographs used in conjunction with the *Exercises* in this book are available in PowerPoint format on the USB Drive provided.

Introduction

How to teach writing to Early Years Foundation Stage (EYFS) and Key Stage 1 (KS1) children and get outstanding results

I have been teaching for a decade and been lucky enough to spend a lot of time working with children aged 4 to 8 years old. During that time, I developed a method which is really easy to teach, creative and actively results in children achieving very high standards in writing. In all cases, whenever I have used these combined methods, I have witnessed the majority of children in my class leaving at the end of the year working at exceeding levels. But more importantly than this, they possessed a love of writing which will benefit them in so many more ways than just being able to compose a sentence.

The techniques I outline are simple to adopt and really work. I feel that in order to be able to achieve things in teaching, it is sometimes really valuable to try a different approach.

Whereas this book has been written with EYFS and KS1 children in mind, the exercises and ideas are fully adaptable for all primary ages.

Now more than ever, it is vital to bring innovation and inventiveness into the curriculum. Teaching children the art of creative writing provides a strong foundation to build upon as they progress through their education into adulthood. Whilst there is a national focus on trying to get more creativeness into the curriculum, there is still an emphasis on achieving results, and an obligation for teachers to accomplish certain standards in the classroom. I found a way to teach English which met these objectives successfully.

However, for myself, teaching writing in this way has always been about more than simply being able to successfully meet data targets. I truly feel that helping children to discover their writing voice at an early age, can lead to increased self-confidence, self-esteem and also links to strong verbal communication abilities. This can, therefore, positively impact on critical thinking skills and the ability to build good relationships.

The significance of becoming an able and keen writer at an early age cannot be emphasised enough. Being able to write skilfully helps children to flourish at school and in everyday life. Writing helps to cultivate a child's cognitive growth, structural capabilities, and the ability to influence others through persuasion. Challenging themselves to generate creative ideas builds the confidence and discipline pupils need to triumph in all matters of life. Children who become competent writers at an early age have been proven to make good progress in all other academic areas.

There are clearly many benefits to children learning to become confident, able and motivated writers at an early age. As well as achieving this by teaching the 'building blocks' of writing – such as phonics and early grammar – it's hugely beneficial to pass on knowledge about what creative writing is and examine this in some detail with children. All too often, schools focus only on the tools of acquiring technical writing ability and becoming proficient in being able to differentiate between fact and fiction at an early age. But teaching pupils the fundamentals of creative writing at an early age can open up a whole spectrum and deliver fantastic outcomes.

It has been proven that the more a child relishes writing, the more frequently they will choose to do this, the greater diversity of writing they will attempt and hence the more progress they will make, leading them to become better writers. Writing benefits children in that it enables them to share their thoughts, handle their emotions and inspires them to dream!

Creative writing inspires children to use their inventiveness and exercise their imaginations. It enhances their capability to come up with alternatives. This extends their thought processes, which can result in greater success in many areas, including problem solving and analysis.

Children often struggle to recognise and articulate how they feel. Through writing, children have a sheltered place to explore. This can be an extremely valuable tool for expressing their feelings. It gives them more openings to assert themselves (and their views) and acquire their 'voice'. These advancements can categorically boost self-assurance.

I have proven that it is possible to deliver a curriculum which is creative and exciting, whilst also helping children to become highly able writers. If I can do it, any teacher can do it!

I do not advocate a type of 'blueprint approach' to writing. My method involves teaching children not only phonics and grammar, but also aspects of creative writing. It is very much about helping children to grasp the fundamentals of storytelling as well as helping them to become aware of wider areas, such as character, plot, setting and even tone! How exciting for young children to take command of these areas, as they set about creating a masterpiece on a blank page, and let their imaginations run wild.

How to Use the Resource

The majority of the photographs featured in the pages of this book are available on the USB Drive as PowerPoints, meaning they can be displayed easily on an Interactive Whiteboard and feature fully in your English lessons. The PowerPoints are labelled by chapter number and name, to make it easy for you to find the photographs you would like to use. The PowerPoints are fully editable so that you can amend the Learning Objective and questions, should you so desire.

Sample PowerPoint slide for Chapter 9 - Teaching about character

Note: If you are unable or not allowed to use the USB Drive, please email info@brilliantpublications.co.uk, telling us when and from whom you purchased your copy.
We will then email you a password and instructions for downloading the files from the Internet.

Section A

Teaching Writing
in the Early Years Foundation Stage

Phonics

Phonics is recommended as the first strategy that children should be taught in helping them to learn to read and write, and has become prominent in UK early years and primary settings. Children need to be taught three main things:

Grapheme-phoneme correspondences

This simply means that they're taught all the phonemes in the English language and ways of writing them down. These sounds are taught in a particular order. The first sounds to be taught are usually: s, a, t, p, i, n.

Blending

Children are taught to be able to blend. This is when children say the sounds that make up a word and are able to merge the sounds together until they can hear what the word is. This skill is vital in learning to read.

Segmenting

Children are taught to segment. This is the opposite of blending. Children are able to say a word, and then break it up into the phonemes that make it up. This skill is vital in being able to spell words.

What makes phonics problematic?

The English Language has around 44 phonemes (sounds), but there are around 120 graphemes or ways of writing down those 44 phonemes (eg, ai, ay, ae, eigh, ey, and a-e, all make the long vowel sound for 'a'). There are only 26 letters in the alphabet and so many graphemes are made up from more than one letter.

Digraphs consist of two letters, for example, 'ch', 'sh', 'th'.

Trigraphs consist of three letters, for example, 'igh'.

The English language can be described as a sort of code, and teaching phonics can help children to crack that code. Children learn the basics first, in the form of the alphabet, and then progress onto the more complicated parts. As children progress from Foundation Stage to Year 3, they move through different phases in their phonic lessons, in which different sounds are taught. In addition to this, they also learn how to spell 'tricky words'. These are the ones which cannot easily be sounded out phonetically, eg, *so, to* and *you*.

There are many different phonics programs, and different schools select the ones which are preferable to them. It is clearly important that phonics is taught in a systematic, fun and 'hands on' way. This involves including different activities in which children learn using all of their senses eg, singing, dancing, making shapes in the air, playing games and using computers, etc. Children then use the knowledge that they have acquired and apply the phonemes in their reading and writing.

Most settings use a mixture of different resources and teaching styles to engage and motivate the children, including magnetic boards and letters, whiteboards and pens, games, flashcards and interactive whiteboard resources. The main thing to remember with regards to these sessions is that multi-sensory activities should be stimulating and engaging but firmly focused on strengthening children's phonic knowledge. They should avoid taking children down a meandering route, only distantly linked to the objective. This means avoiding complex activities that are demanding to manage and take too long to complete, thus diverting the children from focusing on the learning goal.

When it comes to embedding learning, I have found that routine and practice are key. Always have your phonics session take place at the same time each day. The optimum time is the first session of the morning. Phonics is usually the main carpet session activity of the day, and arguably the most important one at this stage in a child's academic life. Holding phonics sessions as the first event of the day avoids having a stop/start approach to the timetable. It allows children to practise the learning which they have acquired in their phonics session in continuous provision areas, which I'll discuss later in the book.

As previously noted, teaching phonics involves introducing children to the graphemes and phonemes in the English language. The usual approach to this is that a new sound is taught every day during the autumn term. Once every sound has been completed, the sounds are then retaught in the spring term. Commonly there is a focus on one grapheme or phoneme on a particular day.

Whereas this is certainly a logical step to take, the pitfall which many teachers fall into is focusing very heavily on a particular sound on one day and then failing to revisit that sound until a whole term later. While it is sensible to teach one sound per day and dedicate a whole session towards that grapheme, this learning is only going into a child's short term memory. Thus, by the time the sound is revisited in the next term, it is likely that the grapheme/phoneme has been forgotten.

The way to avoid this is to ensure that the pupils are secure in knowing the phonic sounds off by heart. My method for this is really simple. I literally just call out the sounds each day and ask the children to write them down on a whiteboard. This takes five minutes. Done on a daily basis, the majority of children are then secure in all Phase 2–5 sounds within a few months at the most and reach the end of the Foundation stage with these sounds fully embedded. In addition, I recommend using either flashcards – or a PowerPoint or slideshow with the graphemes/ phonemes – and zipping through these with the children daily. Ask the children to call out the sounds as they appear. This constant revisiting of the sounds not only embeds learning into long term memory, but it also helps pupils to make links with which graphemes share the same sound. This, in turn, helps with writing and identifying sound families.

The above activity should not be done at the expense of the other phonic activities, which are also important. Rather, they're done on a daily basis as part of the session. It is this regular, constant practice which will ensure that children become secure in being able to write a sound from memory. It not only helps them to be able to automatically write down a sound, it also helps them to segment a word, meaning they're able to write it independently.

Take, for example, the word 'chip'. Many settings provide 'sound mats', and these are certainly a resource which should be available. However, a child should not be overly reliant on these. If this is the case, it hinders the speed at which a writing task can be done and is therefore going to be off-putting to the child. A child may very well be able to segment the word 'ch-i-p' but, having to pull out the sound mat to remind themselves of how the sound 'ch' looks hinders the writing process. How much easier for them to be able to segment, and automatically have the knowledge of how the sound 'ch' in written and just get on with writing the word. How much more satisfying for them. This is a real confidence booster, and also a motivation for children to write as they employ their new knowledge without having to ask for assistance, eg, ask an adult to point out the 'ch' sound on the sound mat.

The reason that this is so important is that, if the phoneme-grapheme links are embedded, children are then able to work independently and get into the 'flow' when writing. Also, they're not relying on using phonic sound cards, which naturally means that they stop and start. It is similar to cooking a meal: if you know what the ingredients are, you can just get on with cooking; if you don't, you have to keep looking up the steps of a recipe.

This method delivers very strong results and will rapidly help children to start writing independently by Christmas.

Continuous Provision

Now that children are gaining the skills to write, the next step is to provide exciting opportunities for them to use and practise these abilities. There are two ways to do this in the Foundation Stage: through continuous provision and through adult-led activities.

Children learn to write in the Foundation Stage through a mixture of adult-directed activities and child-initiated play. For example, they might play at going shopping and 'write' their own shopping list. Alongside play, teachers will inspire children to begin to write through more formal activities. For example, they might draw a picture of a flower and be asked to label the parts, or write their own version of a well-known story like Jack and the Beanstalk.

Points to contemplate

○ Make sure that children have access to their name card, alphabet mat, tricky words and pencil grips.

○ Try to have different types of writing on display around the classroom.

○ Are different languages displayed? Depending on the setting in which you work, this is an important aspect to consider. If there are different languages spoken in your school, think about reflecting this in the types of text which you have on display.

○ It is also really important to have both typed and handwritten labels on displays. Handwriting has become less prominent in the world around us since the digital revolution, but it is still very important to present it in classrooms and not just rely on printed out texts.

○ Is there an alphabet frieze displayed at the child's level? Even though some classrooms have lovely high walls, it is pointless having the alphabet displayed so far above children's eye level.

○ It is crucial that children see adults write every day, not just during teaching activities but also as part and course of conducting matters throughout the day. For instance, making notes, writing messages and adding events to a diary or calendar.

○ Another aspect of this is the importance of modelling writing. This is accomplished through a whole class shared write or during small group activities. It consists of the group segmenting (sounding out) words and then watching as the adult scribes. It can also be done with more involvement from the children if they have their own whiteboards and markers. The more practice they have in participating in this activity, the more quickly they will embed the skills necessary to become confident, independent writers.

○ It is essential to introduce children to a range of types of writing across the year, and make sure that children have opportunities to practise and apply skills taught.

○ Always ask children to talk about their writing, evaluate the progress they're making and discuss their next steps with them. Do not underestimate the significance in children being able to read back what they have written and discuss this.

This section will focus on ideas to encourage children to write independently in the setting, and bring it into their play. It will cover ways to enhance provision and ensure that children are choosing to write.

Areas of provision

Think about your other areas of provision. How many of them contain opportunities to write – not just a clipboard and a pile of A4 paper in the construction area – do you have little books, scrapbooks, a small range of writing materials, prompts for writing in every area?

It is not sufficient to have a well-resourced mark-making/writing table. To increase opportunities further, it is essential that teachers use their skilful expertise and look where else writing can be integrated.

Adding mark-making/writing resources to other areas within the environment will benefit children who are not normally tempted to the mark-making/writing area. Providing an inspiring environment with a wide range of activities that cover all sections of the EYFS will help ensure that all children flurish.

Undoubtedly, as in all things, motivation is the key to encouraging children to write during their independent choosing time. Make sure that you have got writing opportunities in all of your areas, from small world to the maths area. Do you encourage writing in a range of areas (inside and outside) and on the go? Is there an expectation that children will write daily? Do you have well stocked, inviting writing areas? Do you have a system for keeping them well stocked?

Mobile mark-making carriers

Children love these. They can be created from anything. I have used old Pringle's tubs covered in wrapping paper, empty egg cartons and cutlery trays. I fill them with a variety of crayons, pencils, felt-tip pens and add sticky notes, notepaper and small bits of card etc. Leave them scattered around the classroom. Let children help themselves, wander off to an area, and use the resources how they wish. The presentation of the writing opportunity is key here. Should these resources be laid out on a writing table, some children wouldn't be interested. But in creating a different way of accessing the materials, some children will be more inclined to engage. Boys, in particular, are a fan of these. You could even consider making one for every child in the class so that they each have their own personalised mark-making carrier to take around wherever they go in the setting. In the past, I have set this as a 'first week of term' home learning challenge and got parents involved, who loved the idea. Then each child did a 'show and tell' and were able to discuss, with pride, their home-made mobile carrier. This really generated interest from the very start of the year in learning to write and encouraged children to get excited about practising these skills.

Another variation of these are 'writing belts'. You can easily make these out of some old belts with Velcro® and pegs to add on bits and pieces. Bumbags do the same job. These are great for the outdoor area. Small tea trolleys are also a wonderful idea for use outside. This increases 'mobile' opportunities to write as well as the 'static' opportunities that are provided in classroom areas.

Check-list of resources for mark-making/ writing areas inside and outside

○ Don't just rely on plain white paper. Provide assorted sizes, shapes, colours, textures and kinds. Large rolls of paper are fantastic to have unfurled across the classroom floor. The huge sheets of backing paper schools always have in abundance also work well. In the past, I have also used the back of unwanted wallpaper and brown paper packaging.

○ Cardboard is always popular because children see it as being extra special and having more quality. Provide an assortment of colours, textures and thickness.

○ Every now and then, put out some music paper, graph paper or squared paper to add variety.

○ Make sure you have a collection of lined paper pads, notebooks, envelopes, stamps, sticky notes, labels, address books, diaries, registers, forms, headed notepaper, calendars and cards.

○ Ready-made and home-made books work well and tempt children into writing. There are many varieties of these, for example, zigzag, stapled and concertina style.

○ Offer a range of writing tools of different thicknesses – multi-coloured pens, markers, crayons, writing pencils, chalks, coloured pencils, felt-tip pens, gel pens and biros. Don't forget about pencil sharpeners, rubbers, stampers and ink pads, staplers, hole punches, rulers, scissors, sticky tape, glue sticks, paper clips and treasury tags.

Adult-led and Adult-initiated Activities

Ideas to get your EYFS class writing

Here are some ideas that can be used to create opportunities for writing/mark-making and could be carried out either as an adult-led activity, or independently, depending on the children's writing ability, according to the time of the school year.

Signs and notices Get children involved in taking ownership of the classroom. Ask them to create notices and then put them up around the school. Each child could be assigned a notice to create. 'Wash your hands', 'Throw your litter in the bin' and 'Please put the books back on the shelf'. All of these are relevant to life in school and provide a real purpose for writing. Share these as a class and then go and put them up!

Labels This is a similar exercise to the *Signs and notices* task. This time create labels for areas in the classroom. I tend to use sticky notes for this. Let the children have fun putting their labels around the setting. Some of these will be areas which would usually require a label 'felt-tip pens' for instance, on the pots. Other areas will receive a brand new label having never had one before, 'light switch' for example! Children love this activity. I usually leave the labels up for a few weeks or until they start to fall down, so as to let the children enjoy seeing their work for a while and point out their efforts to parents and carers.

Menus Look at some menus on the interactive whiteboard. Then look at some takeaway menus. Talk about favourite foods. Work in groups to create some menus for a role-play takeaway café. This could involve searching on the Internet for different sorts of foods. For instance, if you decide to make a 'Pizza takeaway', look up the different types of pizzas and the sorts of toppings that they include. When the menus have been created, put them into the role-play area for further use. Leave some blank menu templates in the area so that children will be encouraged to repeat the exercise. I usually leave some recipe books in there as well.

Prescriptions Print out some blank prescription forms and let children fill them in. I normally get a teddy bear, and explain that he has got a tummy ache. Then as a group we create a prescription to make him better. This is something along the lines of 'Three cuddles and a kiss.' Or 'A good belly laugh and a drink of hot chocolate'. Children really enjoy the creative side of this activity. I often follow it up by creating a role-play of a vets or doctors' area and leaving blank prescription forms for them to then write their own 'prescriptions'.

Cards These are self-explanatory but children never seem to tire of them. Alongside the regular Christmas, Mother's Day, birthday cards, I inform children of the other 'special days' of the year. There's Earth Day, World Book Day and of course Teachers' Day! However, going one step further and carrying out a simple Internet search reveals that every day is national day of something. The website, *What national day is it today?*, reveals numerous events are marked by a national day every single day. For instance, September 12th: National Ideas Day; National TV Dinner Day, and National Ants on a Log Day. (These are actually a snack in the USA.) Now and then show these to your class. They will delight in hearing about these quirky celebrations and it will provoke great discussion. Leave some blank cards in your writing area and let them create a card to celebrate these little known days. These can then be presented to each other or taken home to loved ones.

Order forms There are various ways to get children excited about filling these out. You can obtain some from catalogues and photocopy them and leave the catalogues out for children to order items to their heart's content.

Application forms Print out some application forms and put up advertisements for different jobs. Maybe it's the line leader of the week. Maybe it's the milk monitor. Have the children help to design the job adverts if you desire. Then help the children to fill out application forms for the position, giving reasons why they should be chosen. Repeat the process each week. Expand on this. Advertise for job roles linked to your fancy dress area. Leave out application forms for joining the police force or becoming a doctor, nurse or fireman. Let the children fill out the forms. The next day, set up a role-play interview, and interview them for the position! This brings in a fantastic opportunity to teach children about questions and statement sentences. Not only that but the children will relish the opportunity to dress up, if they had to earn the right to, by going through the hiring process first! Send home job applications for home learning tasks for upcoming positions throughout the school year, such as *Easter egg distributor* and even *Litter picker*. It's a creative approach and will get parents involved as well.

Blueprints and plans Perfect for using in a construction area or outdoor 'builders yard' role-play. Try to get hold of some blueprints or plans of your own setting. Photocopy them and leave out for children to design their own and then build it out of building bricks.

Instructions These can relate to anything, but work best when working in small adult-led groups. First of all complete a fun activity such as making playdough, baking cookies or planting sunflower seeds. Then write out the instructions step by step. This is a good way to talk about chronological time connectives. Send the instructions home so that children can do the activity with parents.

Letters Always popular, but think outside the box. Ask parents to send in a first class stamp with their children. Request that the children write a letter to their mums and dads. Put them in envelopes and address them. Then take a walk to the letter box and post them. This takes a little organisation, of course, as arranging the walk will require planning in advance, but the children will be beyond excited and it is a lovely surprise for parents to receive the letter in the post.

This activity can be tailored in lots of ways. Write a letter to children in a neighbouring school. Again, this will need to be planned but it doesn't take too much organisation to set up. The children will be thrilled to receive a response.

Follow this up by leaving notepaper on the independent writing table along with envelopes and children will begin to write letters to each other. Set up a letter box in the classroom to be emptied on a weekly basis.

Food orders These lend themselves well to role-play cafés. Use walkie-talkies. Have one child stand at one side of the classroom and the other in the role-play area. Ask one child to 'place an order'. The child in the role-play area then jots down what has been ordered.

Postcards Go for a walk to the local park or the high street. Take photographs. Look at them on your interactive whiteboard. Now print them out and make them into postcards with your children. Prearrange with another school somewhere else in the UK that your class will write postcards and send them to the school. When the reply postcards come back the children will be so excited. You can keep this back and forth chain going on all year.

Draw pictures of your school and make them into postcards. Have your children post them to imaginary characters such as, *Cinderella* or *Jack Frost*. Create response postcards and put them on a noticeboard in the reading area.

Stories and books There are various ways of tackling this. Firstly, blank booklets are always popular. Children love making their own books. Recreate a story that you have read as a book by writing it in their own words. Depending on the time of year they may need to be scaffolded by adults or have word mats in place.

Leave blank booklets in all your areas of provision, even in the garden/outside area. Create baskets of stationery props and refresh these each week. Leave a set of pencils in the basket and see what children come up with.

Make your own class books. Pick a theme and have each child create a page to go into the book. A nice one to start with is a 'Celebration of us'. Each child gets to write about themselves and their favourite things. Add a photograph of the child to go with their writing. Laminate the pages and put it in your book corner. It will be the most popular book in the classroom.

Make an 'And then … ' story. Write a sentence to start a story. Then one by one each child adds the next line. In the end you will have a story of sorts. It may not be completely cohesive but children love this activity. Write all the sentences on one large sheet of card and stick it on the outside of your classroom door for parents to read.

Jokes Begin by setting a home learning challenge. Each child has to learn two jokes to bring into school. Start the session by telling them your own favourites. Then, ask children to recite the jokes they have learned and follow up by scribing them down. Now encourage them to make up their own jokes. They will be ridiculous, and not make any sense, but children won't care and they will find them hilarious. I usually do this around Christmas time and make crackers for the children to take home, stuffed with their jokes.

Notes/messages Make sure you have a well-stocked area with note paper and scraps of paper. I usually raid the recycle bin and slice up unwanted paper and then just leave it stacked up in the writing area. Show the children various sorts of notes on the interactive whiteboard. Get them to write notes to various members of staff with a message from yourself and then deliver them. Recipients could be the Head Teacher, the lunchtime supervisor, the office staff or the caretaker. If you have a teaching assistant, perhaps they can stick around whist the receiver of the note dictates a reply to your message and the children can jot it down. This is writing for a purpose and children enjoy feeling important and grown up. If you have a telephone in your classroom and other staff are game, get them to call you and leave 'messages' for you. The children can answer the phone and write down the message. This can lead to sometimes inaccurate but always lovely notes for you in their attempts to pass on the telephone message.

Invitations What child doesn't love an invitation? Put out some samples on the writing table. Now think of an occasion. It can be anything you like: teddy bears' picnic, Mad Hatter's tea party, assembly for parents or hopscotch competition. Let the children design their own invitations and then write and send them out either to parents or children in another class. The important thing is that the event takes place. Ask the children to come up with ideas for their own events!

Poetry Young children struggle with writing rhyming poetry but given a word bank they can usually construct some sentences that rhyme. I like to use acrostic poems. These work especially well when they're linked to topics or seasons of the year. They're easy for children to get the hang of and usually prove popular for independent writing activities on the writing table. Also, try writing poems using sensory description. Go for a walk in the playground and around school. Have a class discussion about what you saw, heard, felt, smelt and maybe tasted. Scribe a class poem during a shared write. Now get the children to come up with their own ideas. Now set the same task for home learning and ask the children to write a sensory poem about their own home.

Tickets Children could create tickets for a role-play bus or train or tickets for a soccer match. Divide the class into two teams. They each create and sell tickets to the other team for their match. Then go outside and play it.

The potential here is endless. You could have tickets for puppet shows, tickets for singing concerts, tickets for their own nativities, etc.

Receipts Why don't you set up a stall and sell something every Monday morning that the children have made? It could be biscuits or buns. It could be art work. It could be a clay tea light holder. Maybe you could ask for donations of unwanted books and toys from home. Home-made playdough or slime that the children have made is always popular. Rotate which children get to run the stall each week. Another variation on this is to set up a weekly tuckshop. Ask parents to send in donations of food to sell. Children can each bring in a small amount of money. Those running the stall write the receipts upon being given cash. This is not only a meaningful writing with purpose activity, but it also generates a steady stream of income for school funds.

Recipes Ask children what their favourite meals are. Look up the recipes and scribe them down. Make a class cookery book. Cook some of the recipes.

Create your own. What about making a dream dessert? Have children draw this and then write the recipe. This works really well in the messy play area. Children could make the dessert from playdough and write the recipe on a clipboard.

Maps What child doesn't love a map? Make maps of settings in stories that you have read. Make a map of children's route to school. Make a map of a route from the classroom to a pretend door to another world and, of course, the always popular, pirates' treasure map. Print out lots of maps and leave them in the construction area. This activity usually needs little introduction, but children will delight in making their own maps and labelling the areas.

Posters You can make posters for events that are going on in the school calendar and display them around the school. There is always something happening so it could be the upcoming spring concert or enterprise week. Or perhaps it could be a friendly request to *Do not park on the yellow lines in front of the school!* I usually check the newsletter to see what's happening and then get the children involved.

Sign-up sheets This is another really easy method to introduce daily writing for a purpose into your setting. Sign-up sheets are easy to create and can be adopted for a multitude of purposes. What about creating a sign-up sheet for children who want to join in with various activities that you are going to be hosting throughout the day? Skipping contests. Races. Volunteering to go and tidy the PE cupboard! The opportunities are endless. You can also add a comments section, so that children can add on their ideas or questions about the event. For example, when I created a sign-up sheet to go outside and build a snowman, one child wrote in the comments section,

"Can we give him blue bricks for eyes?"

Shopping lists Get the children involved in creating shopping lists of items that you need to purchase in order to carry out upcoming activities in the classroom. Are you going to celebrate Chinese New Year? Make a shopping list of all the ingredients you need to prepare and cook spring rolls. For Mother's Day, make shopping lists for items you need to make bath bombs (after researching online), then make them and give as gifts to mums. I have even involved children in purchasing termly items for the classroom using a supplier's catalogue. You don't need to follow through on all of these, of course, but children love to create a wish list. I leave the catalogues lying around with paper cut into shopping list size and children are always keen to write down items they would like for the classroom.

Bills/invoices I have had a lot of fun with these in the classroom. You can of course get the children to create them for sensible things, such as collecting dinner money or milk money, but you can also invoice for things that can be paid for with non-monetary currency. What about creating an invoice to send home for mums and dads, that invoices them for a picture that their child has created that requests payment in the form of a cuddle? These are popular with parents.

Captions I usually introduce this activity by photocopying pages from a 'Book of the week' and asking children to create a caption or sentence to describe what is happening in the picture. Once they get the hang of it you can take this in so many directions. I like to ask parents to send in photographs from home, especially 'candid shots'. Then I get the children to write a caption. Of course, we do not often know what is exactly happening in the photograph so this can be really fun. I have a display board to show off the products of these activities and they're really popular with parents.

I have used this as a home-learning activity by taking a photograph of the whole class in the midst of an activity, maybe PE or singing or in the playground. It is a picture that represents a moment in time. I send it home and ask the children to caption it with their parents' help. These can lead to some really amusing results.

Registers This a really self-explanatory one. Children love to pretend that they're the teacher. You can take it one step further and have the children create their own members' only clubs. This links in nicely to the sign-up sheet activities for instance, I had a gardening club recently and the children selected the 'chair' of the club who would create and keep the register. The children will come up with all sorts of themes for clubs: unicorn, superhero, table tennis …

Diaries I like to have the children keep a diary over the course of a week every half term. This is a lovely way for them to record what is happening and learn the days of the week. I often set a home-learning challenge linked to keeping a diary over the holidays.

Instructions As well as writing instructions for actual activities, it's also fun to get the children to write instructions for imaginary events: *How to grow a chocolate tree* and *How to teach a pony to sing*, have been some of the ones that I have used in the past. The fact that they're silly and fun really capture the children's imagination and before too long they start to come up with their own ideas. I have often collected these and made a class book called 'Instructions on life' and again, it is always one of the most popular books on the classroom shelf.

Licences You can create a licence to ride a bike in the playground or a licence to drive the pedal car or go-kart in the playground. But you can come up with other things that need licences. What about creating a licence to walk to the Head Teacher's office alone? Or, a licence to deliver a message to the teacher next door? This gives children a feeling of responsibility, and they love collecting them. Parents in the past have sent in toy wallets and purses for children to keep their licences inside.

Scoresheets You can keep score of football games in the playground, skittles and hopscotch. Who's got their coat on and zipped up, the fastest? How many books have the children read this week? Who spent the longest time on their artwork? I tend not to focus on winning and losing, but rather taking part and with an emphasis on participation and times that something has occurred. This makes it less of a competitive writing activity and more about recording information.

Valuing Writing in the Classroom and Getting Parents Involved and On-board

If you want children to value writing it is really important to hold it in high-esteem. Arguably, writing is the most difficult skill which children acquire during their time in the Foundation stage. Therefore, I have always felt that it is important to give it the due recognition that it needs. In order to progress sufficiently, it requires that children obtain knowledge about phonics and how the English language works. Key points are: understanding about writing from left to right, finger spaces and also thinking about capital letters and full stops. On top of this, children have to get to grips with letter formation and the difference between upper and lower case letters.

For this reason, it takes time and practice to progress. It's my belief that it is therefore justified to prioritise writing in some aspects of your practice. For example, children love 'show and tell'. It's a fantastic activity, and it helps children to develop in many ways. They gain confidence in speaking in front of their peers, they're able to be the centre of attention – which makes them feel special – and they're practising their speaking and listening abilities. However, there is only so much time in a week. I looked at all the benefits that 'show and tell' brings and decided to replace it with a more 'writing' centric approach. I therefore told children that we would start every day with a session in which, if they had produced any writing at home they could bring it in and show myself and the rest of the class. They would then have the opportunity to discuss the work, answer questions and read it out loud. In return they would receive a sticker. Children would always receive a round of applause upon reading their work out loud. It also helped them with the skill of re-reading their work, which is something that is often overlooked in its importance. The work would go on the wall. Should parents want to stay and watch this they were more than welcome and encouraged to do so.

The benefits of this approach were numerous. Suddenly children were motivated to go home and write. Parents were getting involved and many children wanted to have some writing to bring in every day. This meant that the skills which they were acquiring were being practised every day at home, and not just in the setting. Not only that, but they were encouraged to be as creative as possible and therefore were generating stories, newspaper articles, letters, factual accounts and recounts of days out. This is one of the most impactful aspects of my practice and, coupled with the tactics which I have already described above, it led to children making solid progress within writing. Yet, and some would argue even more importantly, it led to children becoming excited and motivated to write, which, as a teacher, I felt was one of the most valuable impacts that I could make.

Most Foundation units hold a presentation for parents in order to communicate the ways in which they will be teaching their children to read and write, as well as sharing ideas about how they can help at home. I have found that it is valuable to help parents to understand that they can play a key role in helping their child to enjoy writing. I always stress that the key to success is to make writing both fun and purposeful. I usually create a writing booklet to send home to parents, and also post information onto the school website. If you have a school blog, update it regularly for parents with ideas for them to use at home.

Establishing a writing culture at home will help it to become a part of normal life for their child. Urge parents and carers to let children see them writing frequently to help underpin how

---

significant writing is to day-to-day life. Explain to parents how they can become a writing role model by taking every chance they get to write at home. This can be as simple as writing out a shopping list, birthday cards or creating a family noticeboard for everyone to put notes on.

Ask parents to make it easy for children to write whenever the mood takes them. They can accomplish this by providing a container of writing materials for them to use at home. Suggest that they stock the box with pens, colouring pencils and notepads and take time every week to use the box as a family. They could play games that involve writing, such as hangman or word searches, or add in interesting objects which they could ask their child to weave into a story.

Parents know best where their children's interests lie, so encourage parents to give them a reason to write about it. If their child is a fan of football, they could encourage them to write a match report after a football game to share with their teacher. Or, after a holiday or family event, they could encourage their child to email their grandparents to tell them all about it, including fun photos and website links too. In the past, some parents in my class have allowed their children to send emails to other children in my class. This will need to be set up and monitored by the parents using their own personal email accounts, but it is another way to get children excited about communicating and a valid form of writing.

Building Vocabulary and 'Photo of the Day'

The more words children know, the better writer they will be. Take every chance you can to encourage conversation and verbal communication with your class in order to increase their vocabulary. I have always chosen to use a rich vocabulary when addressing children and have not opted to use simplified words. For instance, a child is equally capable of learning and understanding the use of the word 'communicate' as they are the word 'talk'. Varying your word choices, and including sophisticated synonyms when you address children, will help them to build their lexicon. This will eventually soak through into their written communication.

Good writers are also sound readers. Reading assists children to experience other voices, genres and ways of writing. It also aids them to increase their vocabularies, find stimulation and develop their understanding of language and the world around them. Take advantage of your school library and encourage parents to visit their own local library with children. Provide a wide range of opportunities to listen to stories. This means not only reading a whole class story on a daily basis and listening to them read on a one-to-one basis each week, but also providing other methods. Talking stories are fantastic. I still always create a 'listening station' with a CD player, headphones and books on CD. Alternatively, children could listen to stories on websites. Encourage children to record themselves reading books, then transfer these onto CDs for their classmates to listen to. I set this as a challenge for children to do at home, should they wish to do so. Parents in the past have recorded the results on their mobile phones and emailed in the sound bites. I then created a file on the class computer which children could access, listen to and enjoy the stories read by their classmates.

Play word games, such as 'hangman', anagrams and 'I spy'. Once you have played these as a whole class, children will soon start to bring these into their independent play.

Consider having a 'word of the week'. I like to choose a high-level synonym for instance, 'precipitation' instead of 'rain'. Make a conscious effort to use the word throughout the week and encourage the children to do the same. Create a 'WOW' display and keep adding to it. By the end of the year the children will have acquired over 38 words.

Topic words are another great way to boost vocabulary. Depending on what your classroom theme is, you can create word banks and print these out for writing tables as well as displaying them on walls. I always send these home as well to keep parents involved. Email them or add them to the school blog or website or simply print out a copy and send them home with the children.

Superlatives are a really fun way to quickly add words to children's vocabulary. In the past I have created a 'superlative beanstalk' which the class have added to until it stretches high up to the ceiling. Each leaf has a different word, such as 'fantastic' and 'marvellous'. I usually do this as a whole class activity, and it takes a whole afternoon but the results are worth it. I then create a picture of a beanstalk with blank spaces on the leaves and ask children to scribe down their favourite superlatives on it and send it home for more suggestions as a home learning activity.

One of the most popular activities in my classroom is always 'picture of the day'. I have traditionally done this during milk and snack time. We gather on the carpet and children examine a picture on the interactive whiteboard. There are hundreds of websites which provide daily photographs. One of my favourites is the National Geographic website but a simple Internet search will throw up many more. At the start of the year, I just encourage children to contribute their thoughts about the photograph or picture. I then read them the information which accompanies the picture. This is a great way to cover news topics and build in a global learning approach to your class.

After a few weeks I introduce the concepts of *Who*, *What*, *Why*, *Where* and *When* and of course *How* (the 5 Ws and 1H). Now, when children discuss the picture, I want them to do it with a view to having these questions in mind. I usually give the children 10 minutes to talk about the picture with the person next to them. We then feedback as a whole class, and I scribe ideas onto the whiteboard in relation to the questions we have been considering. Of course, there is no right or wrong answer because we have just been looking at possibilities linked to the picture before the class are aware of the background information. I gradually build on this approach until we are eventually crafting a story from each picture on a daily basis.

This approach really gets children into the mind-set of becoming 'storytellers'. It's hugely beneficial because, once children have grasped the skill of applying these sorts of thoughts to an idea, or object, they can take this skill and use it in many different ways. Being able to tell a story orally is a building block to being able to write their own stories, so it's a terrific way to help children acquire this ability. It also assists children's critical thinking across the entire curriculum.

Storyteller

Who is this girl? Where is she going? Why is she alone?
What is in the woods waiting for her to discover?
When did this happen?

Other ways to orally build storytelling abilities

Paper finger cone puppets

Home-made finger cone puppets are particularly helpful for inventing dialogue between characters. You can make some rapid cone-shaped finger puppets out of paper or card and resources in your art areas. Create any characters you like. Fairy tale characters always go down well; equally popular are family members. Of course, you can also link them to your current topic or book of the week. Scaffold children in using these puppets by working in small groups, demonstrating how to create dialogue between the characters in different scenarios, such as "You ate my slice of pizza …" or "My favourite thing to do after school is …". You can also use the 5 Ws and 1H system as a prompt. For instance, "What is your character doing?" or "Describe who your character is in this story?"

Story cubes

You can create your own story cube by making a cardboard cube and then sticking some opening lines onto each side. These can be used to provide some inspiration on how to start a story. I introduce these to my class in small group activities but also like to make some linked to topics. I leave them lying around the classroom for children to discover and use in their play or to encourage them to make up oral stories to tell to each other. A really great area to place these is in your small world continuous provision. You already have a ready-made setting and characters, so the addition of a story cube is a fantastic way to enrich this resource.

Draw a picture game

This one is a pleasing small group activity. Everybody begins by drawing any picture they desire onto a piece of paper. Then they swap their drawings with the individual next to them. That child then tells a story based on the drawing they have. This is a great game for connecting with each other and develops children's visualisation skills as well as interpretation skills!

Free-writing Exercise

This simple activity has made all the difference during my time in teaching EYFS children with regards to how quickly they become skilled in writing independently. All it involves is children spending 10 minutes a day drawing a picture, and then adding some writing. As the year goes along, they're taught different methods to build up the amount of writing produced. I have made it a daily event. Not only does it help children to develop their fine motor skills in producing the drawing, but it also encourages them to use their imagination. When it comes to adding writing, the children use the phonic knowledge that they have acquired.

At the start of the year, I work with the children in small groups, and they're given an instruction about what to draw. For instance, 'Red Riding Hood', and we complete a shared write about the picture. This enables the children to practise writing captions and then sentences. It is a fast activity, but it is solidifying the ability to get a sentence onto paper.

As the year progresses and children have become able to recall all the phonics sounds, are proficient in segmenting words and more able to construct a sentence independently, they're simply told to create a picture of their choice and add a sentence. I let them do this independently and then, when they show it to me, I read what they have written. At the end of the day, they take the picture home. This means they always have something to take home at the end of the day. Children adore taking home their artwork and writing. Practice makes perfect. It is a simple, small practice that can easily be adopted into your day-to-day routine but it will make all the difference when it comes to the proficiency with which children are able to write at the end of the school year.

I don't always stay in the classroom. I like to go to other areas in the school to vary the environment. A few times a week, I go with my class to the library and complete this task with children there. Other times we go into the hall, and the children lie on the floor on their stomachs and do their picture.

Section B

Teaching Writing in Years 1 and 2

English Sessions

Once pupils have moved into Years 1 and 2, it is ideal for the phonics session to take place before the English Literacy session because children are then able to practise the skills which they have been revising.

As a primary teacher, I highlight to pupils that people write because we have something to say. Therefore, when they write it is because *they* themselves have something to say. I'd maintain that, not only is it essential that young children appreciate the approaches we use to communicate on paper, but it's also important for them to write with an authority that comes from speaking as *themselves*.

Half of this task entails aiding children to grasp that which they need to comprehend in order to be able to put pen to paper: learning how to spell and use grammar accurately. A teacher's role, I believe, is to also aid all pupils to find the confidence to communicate and share ideas, and understand that their ideas are as valid as anyone else's. Consequently, I'd argue that if the vocal voice is seen as an essential part in advancing a child's self-assurance, then the written voice should also be fostered with the understanding that it can also impact on a child's self-confidence. We are all born with a voice, and we start acquiring it as soon as we can converse verbally. Therefore, it stands to reason that as soon as children attain the required tools to write, that they should also be given ownership of their writer's voice and encouraged to recognise that it should be a true expression of who you are. I believe that this assists children to ascertain who they are as a person.

Children should be championed to nurture their own writing voice, not try to shape it into something other than their genuine self. This means that children should be provided occasions to write in a conversational, or informal tone, use jargon which they would when talking and be taught to 'speak' to a reader. This means specifically making children conscious that they're writing for somebody to read their work, and that the reader will develop a view of the writer. All too frequently, this isn't conveyed to children. It is taken for granted that they'll understand this notion without it being explicitly explained. I've discovered that, through shared 'whole class writes' and active demonstrations on how to write using our 'own way of talking', children in my own classes have then been able to work autonomously, with self-assurance in their own style, and not feel as though they have to assume a tone that doesn't reflect who they are. Without being given this reassurance beforehand, even in young children's prose, sentences are often written in a way in which the child would never speak verbally.

Children as young as 5 or 6 are able to understand the following idea: the way in which they engage with their parents in their homes is unlike how they communicate with a teacher in the classroom, and again, unlike the way in which they chat with their friends in the playground and this plainly underscores my earlier statement. Through pointing this out to children, they are able to access these distinctive areas of their conscious selves when they write. One way of accomplishing this is an activity which consists of debating a picture. I used this exercise with a Year 1 class of 6-year-olds and we considered a photograph of a plate of fish, chips and peas. The children worked in pairs to contemplate what they might say about this if the plate was positioned in front of them, depending on whom they were with at the time. To parents, they might say: "I'm not eating that, you know I hate peas." To a dinner lady, they might say: "I'm full." To their classmate, they might say: "Peas are disgusting." Children then went on, over the course of the week, to write three different letters about this imagined dinner, to three different people in their lives. It helped children to appreciate how they switch their attitude, and approach, depending on whom they're talking to, and that this applies to both spoken and written words. This underpinned

How to Achieve Outstanding Writers in the Early Years Foundation Stage and Key Stage 1
© Brilliant Publications Limited

the notion that a writer's voice can be shifting, but they can still 'own' their written words, even when the reader changes.

I teach children that, occasionally, the finest writing can be virtually intuitive. This means just sitting down, and allowing the process to occur, without overthinking or questioning every word. This is what happens when we have vocal conversations. We simply allow the words to emerge. This can also take place with writing.

When working in Foundation stage settings, I'd set children a 10 minute daily task every afternoon, in which they drew a picture about whatever they chose, and wrote something about it (after being given a sheet of blank white paper). This was done every day, over the course of the year, and was totally autonomous work. In the morning, short phonic sessions were taught to embed the tools of writing. I also would lead small, adult-led guided writes in the morning, of no more than 10 minutes. The results were extraordinary. It not only made it possible for children to get to grips with the dexterity of early grammar, but it also produced motivated writers, who took ownership of what they were expressing and permitted them to have faith in their written voice. This exercise delivered a starting point for the writing, whilst also allowing a freedom of choice. These pictures, and the writings created, ranged from 'Cat on a flying carpet', to 'Spiderman driving a bus' to 'Princess making a cake'. No matter the topic, the outcome of doing this regularly for a year constantly led to the majority of children departing my Foundation Stage class working at levels of Year 1 children. The daily routine allowed them to embed key phonics and grammar. The children becoming capable of using these tools independently meant that I could teach the next steps (which was the grammar of the next year group). The quantity and standard of writing would build up over the course of a year.

I've also done this exercise with 5- and 6-year-olds in Year 1. I build on the exercise so that children received a sheet of paper with a top section for a drawing, and lines to write several paragraphs about the drawing. Children were told to write whatever they had in mind. This led to rich language choice and interesting content. Towards the end of the year, I sometimes take away the drawing aspect of the exercise and progress straight to the writing after having a whole class discussion about a prop or a photograph.

I carried out this exercise daily for the course of the school year. During these sessions, the focus was on simply writing what came to mind. At times, children would go back and edit work during another session, but not always, although this also played a part in developing technical skills.

I firmly believe that taking chances and experimenting with pedagogical practice means that primary teachers are better able to encourage and assist children to develop their voices as writers.

Re-reading what one has written is a key part of the National Curriculum in Key Stage 1. The foremost purpose of this is for children to understand that what they have written needs to be legible, and understandable, for the reader. However, this can also be a useful tool in evolving and identifying their own writing voice.

My way of motivating children to want to learn involved showing them videos of adults doing exciting job roles, such as astronauts, scientists, journalists, pilots, doctors etc. I discussed how being able to read and write would enable them to do many different vocations when they grew up, and so it was important to work hard now. I found that this was very effectual, and that children were able to grasp that they were actually working hard and investing in 'themselves'. Too often, children have the viewpoint that they have to do work because the teacher makes them. By familiarising them with the concept that they were working for their future selves, enabled them to begin a dedication to their education which is rare for young children.

Incorporating *Actively* Teaching Creative Writing into your Practice

I assert that *actively teaching creative writing techniques*, as part of English lessons, for KS1 children is highly beneficial. This is not a requirement in the National Curriculum for these children, but what a difference it made when I began to vigorously go out of my way to include it in my English lessons.

Stories

School children are exposed to stories through initially being read to and then by reading independently. Schools, however, work under the assumption that children absorb, and intuitively feel, what 'seems like a story' and how to create their own.

Children soak up stories through listening to them, and almost unconsciously they begin to understand the basics of plot and structure. But taking dedicated time to explain how these ideas work, and also inform children how they can consciously use creative writing techniques in their writing, makes a momentous impact. It doesn't take a great deal of time or effort to do this, but it enriches children's learning experiences massively. It also equips them, as writers, with an array of tools at their disposal which they will grow skilled at understanding and utilising as they progress through the education system.

This allows children to be able to respond to writing a story in an instinctual way. It is a different approach to current popular strategies, in which children learn a traditional story off by heart, and then write their own story by tweaking and changing aspects of the original so that they have a watered down version, a type of blueprint.

Not only do I teach children creative writing tools, but I also comment on how they can use these in their independent writing. Thus character creation, setting, tone and pace could all be commented on by all teachers, as a matter of course, whilst feeding back on young children's work. Focusing on these aspects of writing and not just on building blocks such as 'correct spellings' will help to create confident and able writers, who have ownership of their writing voices.

The importance of creative writing in advancing children's cognitive and communication skills cannot be undervalued. When they're writing, children become creators. Creative writing assists children in being able to translate their thought processes in a coherent and articulate manner. When children come up with characters and storylines, they logically start to explore feelings, values, hopes and fears. This can assist in building empathy.

With these compelling motives in mind, it is difficult to defend not making creative writing a significant area of Key Stage 1 English coverage. Writing opportunities should undoubtedly be enjoyable and children should have occasions to choose their own focuses and approaches to writing as I have discussed in the use of 'producing a picture a day' method.

What is a story and why are they so important? How to embrace oral storytelling in your classroom

Stories are a central part of our societies and culture. We are surrounded by stories in our day-to-day existence. Books, films, music, painting, art, news are just a few examples. The impact of storytelling is reflected in all parts of our lives. It expresses our values and ethics, our desires and dreams, and our fears. In truth, storytelling helps to define and connect our humanity. Humans are the only animals that create and tell stories.

We take it for granted that children love stories. But we rarely talk to them about why we tell these. But, of course, it's fascinating for them to understand a little about how it all began! I find that doing this is a fantastic starting point for teaching English to KS1 children.

Traditionally, oral stories have been passed down from generation to generation. Nobody knows when the first story was really articulated. We tend to imagine that it occurred in a dimly lit cave around a glimmering fire. Whereas we cannot establish 'where?' the first story occurred, but we can discuss 'why?'. It is widely accepted that the foundation of storytelling began as a justification for failure, used to calm fears or doubts of those who lived long ago.

People found them interesting and entertaining and an art form was born.

A good storyteller was eternally valued. Their stories were exchanged with others in far off lands because when people travelled they took with them their tales. And, when they returned, they fetched back new fables of exotic places and people.

Discuss with children in your class all the reasons why we tell and write stories. We do it to entertain and to nurture artistic expression. We do it to explore and practise the purposes and standards of writing. It helps us in our search for identity and to understand each other. It inspires us to use our imagination.

Oral storytelling

Oral storytelling is an important art form and skill. It is one which is gradually being lost as we live in an age of 'streaming' and 'binge-watching'. Encouraging children to become oral storytellers is a fantastic way to help to keep this tradition alive. One way I do this is to have a 'storyteller of the day'. Before the register each morning, a child will tell a story of their choosing. They can make it up on the spot or practise it at home. Children adore this activity. I usually have a 'storyteller hat' to make it even more of a special event. Film it and put it on your blog or website for parents to enjoy.

Exercise

Who do you think this storyteller is?

Who is his audience? What is his story about?

How to Achieve Outstanding Writers in the Early Years Foundation Stage and Key Stage 1

Teaching about Character

Key Stage 1 children are able to identify that a character in literature is whoever appears in that story. In order to write a story, children obviously have to have someone to write about. However, there is so much more to this concept which is beneficial for children to get to grips with.

I usually start by doing a character study linked to a book which we have been reading in class. Look at external and internal characteristics. Make a list of them. Too often, children focus on what a character looks like but don't think about personality aspects, and this is what makes stories interesting. Take this even further! Talk about how in stories there are often *goodies* and *baddies,* but in real life, it doesn't actually work like that. We all have traits that we should be proud of and things that we have to work on. That's because people are not perfect! For example, look at *Jack and the Beanstalk*.

Jack's characteristics:

External: Boy, brown hair, athletic, blue eyes.

Internal: Brave (he climbed the beanstalk).

Loving (he wants to take care of his mother).

Clever (he tricked the giant).

Untrustworthy (he ran off with the harp).

Mean streak (he chopped down the beanstalk after stealing the giant's money. *Killing the giant!)*

Yes, Jack had his reasons for his behaviour. We will look at character motives later on.

Character study and character generation

I follow up this teaching input by asking children to do two character studies.

The first is of themselves: give them a photograph of themselves and ask them to create a mind map which lists all of their external characteristics, as well as their likes and dislikes. In completing this activity, children will really start to get a feel for the complexities of character creation. Next, get them to complete a character study from a character in a picture book that the class has shared.

Follow this up by asking children to create their own character. Ask your child, who is going to be in the story? How do they want their readers to feel about each character? Draw the character on paper and add character traits, focusing on both internal and external characteristics and also thinking about less desirable traits as well as endearing ones.

You could make a table for them to help them categorise their thoughts, with these headlines:
- Name of character
- Relationship to other characters
- What s/he looks like (external)
- Behaviour (internal)

Once pupils have thought about these characters I ask them to write a monologue beginning with the line, 'It's the middle of the night and I cannot fall asleep and all because … ' What is this new character anxious about, or perhaps, looking forward to? What have they done that led to them feeling this way or what will they have to do? Children always engage with this task and it produces energised and encouraging writing.

Generating a convincing character is one of the most demanding challenges in writing a piece of fiction. There are plenty of stories in which the characters are boring, or replicas of the same characters we've met in lots of stories previously.

Readers want characters who are as distinctive and multifaceted as real people. Children are more than capable of understanding this concept. Not only does it make creating a character a lot more interesting but it also helps them to think about personal and social aspects of their own selves. Children at this age are still developing their personalities and it is a way to help them recognise traits that they possess and to have ownership.

Characterisation

and Character Writing Exercise

Create a character together as a class.

Choose a name and then ask for ideas about the appearance of this character.

How old are they?

What is their occupation?

Once you have covered the internal and external characteristics, talk to pupils about how character profiles can lead to plot development.

Ask them:

* What challenges does this character face?

  * What does this character desire more than anything else?

    * What obstacles are in the way of this character's desire?

      * What situation might cause the character to react in an interesting way?

Goals

This is a good time to introduce children to the concept that a character must always want something. Without that, there is no story. They may, or may not, obtain their desire in the story, but they need to try to get it. This is something for children to bear in mind as they go on to craft their own stories as they progress through school. It is a sophisticated concept, but in being aware of it, children are better able to consider this when they're plotting stories.

A protagonist can have a simple goal, like going to the park after school to play with friends, or it could be a significant goal, like saving the world from a supervillain. Almost every story involves a goal at the heart of the plot. This is a core element of storytelling and so, in enabling children to become familiar with this concept, you are teaching them the fundamentals of how stories work.

As you share books with your class during carpet sessions or end of day story time and as you listen to children read individually, begin to discuss the characters in the book. Think about their characteristics and their goals. The more adept that children become at identifying these, the more they will start to bring these concepts into their own stories.

Tips to help children create characters:

- Ask children to think of all the people in their lives, or whom they have seen on TV. Take their firmest and most attention-grabbing qualities and behaviours and assign them to characters.

- Talk to the children about what they want to be when they grow up? Pilot or actress or doctor? Use these as inspiration for their characters.

- Think about details. What do they wear? How do they do their hair? Does he wear a leather jacket or a suit? Does she sing in the car or is she always looking worried? These are the things which make a character really interesting.

- What about the character's hobbies? Even if a character's interests aren't linked immediately to the plot, they will enhance it and make the character more believable.

Mannerisms and gestures are always great to include. Encourage children to assign to his or her characters their own distinctive physical behaviours, such as biting their nails or clicking their tongue.

Character strengths, skills and assets

Characters need to possess strengths, skills and assets so that they're able to endure the different challenges that a story inevitably throws at them. These can be personal strengths, like resilience or trustworthiness, or they can be abilities, like karate. Material assets, such as owning a bicycle or a computer, might come in useful in the story. Talk to children about this concept. As you read stories to the class, talk about character flaws and strengths as you progress through the book. This will help children become used to analysing stories and then, in turn, using this information to generate their own work.

Character flaws and weaknesses

A character should also have imperfections and weaknesses because nobody is perfect and that would be boring. These make characters relatable. Flaws and weaknesses interfere with the characters' progress toward their goals and provide setbacks for the plot. Readers want to see characters succeed, but if it comes after a few failures, caused by the characters' own flaws and weaknesses, this makes the character more endearing. Talk to children about this notion and explain why it is important that a character has a balance of flaws and weaknesses.

Exercise

Watch the movie, Peter Pan.

As a class, make a list of the strengths, skills and assets of Tinkerbell, the fairy.

- she's clever
- pretty
- knows magic

Now list her flaws and weaknesses.

- she's jealous (of Wendy)
- prone to sulking
- she can't talk (but as an audience we still love her)

Now ask the children to create their own fairy character. Come up with a list of flaws, weaknesses as well as their skills, assets and strengths.

External conflict

It's only interesting to read about characters' working toward a goal if attaining it takes great effort.

External conflicts make it complicated for the characters to accomplish their goals. The external conflict might be the cause of the goal (a bad witch wants to turn everyone into frogs, so we must defeat her). However, external conflict can also interfere with the goal (the protagonist wants a wand and her best friend wants the same one. They spend so much time arguing over this that the witch gets away).

Conflict Exercise

Read 'Snow White and the Seven Dwarves'
with your class.

Have a discussion and list all the external conflicts in the story.

– The Queen wants to kill Snow White because the mirror tells her that Snow White (and not the Queen) is the fairest person in the land.

– The Queen finds out that Snow White has not been killed, so she decides to kill her herself.

– Snow White sleeps for a long time.

Now, do a shared class write. Ask the children to pick one of the dwarves. Create a story about the dwarf. He must have a goal and something must initially get in the way of him obtaining that goal – the conflict. After you have completed this exercise as a class, ask the children to work in groups to create their own stories and act them out. Then go and write them.

Internal conflict

Internal struggles compel characters to make complicated choices. They often must choose from bad, or worse, options and the right choice almost always involves a significant sacrifice.

Conflict Exercise

Create a character with your class about a boy who owns a dog. The dog is pining for a lost ball. The boy suddenly remembers that the dog buried it in the garden last summer. But now his mother's sunflowers are growing over that spot and she is so proud of them. He wants to make his dog happy again, but he doesn't want to upset his mother by digging up the plants.

What does he do?

Ask the children to write their own ending to the story.

Conflict Exercises

Conflict is what makes a story compelling and it can be created in the most unexciting situations.

List some of these normal situations on the whiteboard and discuss with your class how a character can deal with both internal and/or external conflict if placed in the situation.

Character placing an order at McDonald's – Perhaps the character has forgotten their purse and can't pay. Maybe someone cuts in line. Maybe they have forgotten what the person they came with wanted and order the wrong thing. What if they're too shy to talk to the person taking the order? What if they do not want cheese on their burger but can't pluck up the courage to tell the cook?

Character doing the washing up – Maybe they have run out of washing-up liquid, or the water isn't warm enough. Do they drop a plate and break it and then feel too worried to tell the person they live with? What if one person wants to do the washing-up but always gets stuck drying?

The purpose of this exercise is to show that conflict is possible in run-of-the-mill life and it can be used to create an interesting and compelling story out of any occasion. Now you have generated the ideas, let the children go and write a story.

Character Exercises and Story Starters

Missing person Put an extra chair in your classroom and then add a name of a child not in your class to the register, let's say 'Sarah'. Ask the children where Sarah is today. Point to her empty chair. Insist that they tell you where she is. Arrange for a teaching assistant to make up a reason why Sarah isn't in school. Disagree with her and claim that you heard differently. Ask if anyone knows anything else. Ask who was the last person to see Sarah. Children will soon realise this is a game. Agree that Sarah is missing. Make a list on the whiteboard of her external and internal characteristics. Then think about why she might not be in school. Conflict! Make some 'missing' posters for Sarah and then ask children to write a story about where she is today.

Super pet   Of course, not all characters are human. Ask children to create a character who is a super pet. Still ask for internal and external characteristics, as well as their strengths and weaknesses. Who does the super pet help and why?

The lifeguard who was afraid of water   This is a great exercise for exploring internal and external conflict. Why is the lifeguard afraid of water? Has it always been that way? What happens when they see someone start to drown, is there anyone else around who can help? What are the traits of the lifeguard that will impact how they react? Write this as a shared write and a whole class activity before asking children to create their own stories.

Waiting for the train   Who is this man? Where is he going on the train?

Peter Piper picked ... This is a famous tongue twister which explores alliteration. Choose a letter and create another version as a class altogether. Now ask children to create their own character using alliteration. For example, Happy Harry had a hat. Now write a story about Happy Harry and his hat.

The most famous person in the world Ask children to create a character who becomes famous overnight. What did they do to become so famous? What are they like? Are they happy or sad about it? What are their characteristics that help them to cope with fame? What happens next?

Magic or something else? Who is she and what's happening here?

Crazy scientist   This person has just come up with a new invention which will change the world. What is it? What will they do with it? Tell us about the scientist.

Confused Connie   What is she so confused about? Tell us about her personality and then tell us how she stops being confused.

What do you want to be when you grow up and why?   Ask children to pretend that they're that person already and write about a day that they just spent as that future person. Concentrate on goals.

Seven left   Tell us about this cat. Who is she and why has she only got 7 out of her 9 lives left?

Twilight adventurer   Who is this boy? Where is he going and why?

Imaginary friend Ask children to invent a character who is their imaginary friend who only they can see. They don't have to be human! What are their goals? What are their mannerisms and gestures like?

Why did the chicken cross the road? Tell children to pretend to be an investigator assigned to find out what the chicken was doing. What was the chicken like and what were his goals and motivation for crossing the road?

Pirate captain   Write about where they went to dig up their treasure and what they did with it next.

Teaching about Setting

Setting is as essential to a story as is character and plot and being able to create a vivid setting is a central component of storytelling. The setting of a story establishes where and when events take place.

Show your class a selection of picture books with which they're familiar and then list all the settings in the stories. Discuss how the setting of the story consequently drives the action and so children need to acquire the ability to create vivid settings in their writing.

How do they accomplish that? Well, settings are largely established through the use of description.

However, it is also worth demonstrating that action and dialogue can also be utilised to transport readers into a story world. Characters interact with the world around them. As well as this, they talk about it. This is another strategy that writers can use to establish their setting.

Reference to setting can therefore be incorporated into action and dialogue, as long as it's natural to the story. Helping children to become proficient at doing this is a really good way to help them to become confident and able in communicating details about their story worlds.

Whole Class

Exercise 1

Describe a place to your class. I usually prepare
a written description on the whiteboard. Avoid naming it but read
it out to the children. Now ask them to try to guess what the place is.
I like to do this with the school canteen as the setting.

"The room is packed with hungry children.
The blue and green chairs are squashed around the tables.
The purple walls need to be repainted, but the display boards have
some beautiful artwork from Year 2 on them."

Now put the children into pairs and get them to describe
settings to each other that they will be familiar with
and ask their partner to guess the place.

Whole Class

Exercise 2

Prepare a written description on the whiteboard which uses action
and dialogue to show a setting. For instance:
"Kick the ball to me," shouted Peter as he ran over the concrete. He
bumped into some of the other children by accident. The ball came his way
but, before he got chance to kick it, the bell rang and he had to go inside. He
grabbed the box of leftover milk to take with him as he went.
Ask the children to name the location. Now put the children into pairs
and get them to describe settings that they will be familiar with using
action and dialogue. It can take a bit of practice for children to get the
hang of doing this, but they will soon become well acquainted
with it and start to use this method in
their own writing.

Senses

The senses of smelling, tasting, hearing, feeling and sight, are what help us identify objects and places. It helps the reader picture themselves actually being in the story and helps the story come to life.

Other considerations

Setting just doesn't refer to locale or the immediate area in which the story occurs, for example, country, city, house or school. So whereas, description of location is important, there are other components which fall under the umbrella of 'setting' which children need to be aware of.

Time   The time of year might be important in the story. This includes the seasons but also encompasses holidays, such as Christmas and Halloween or a character's birthday. Time of day can sometimes be key to a story. Scenes occur during various times of the day or night. It can be beneficial for children to be mindful of these details and include them in their stories.

Weather and climate   Climate is connected to the geography of a setting and can influence events and characters in the story and assist in bringing a story world to life. Is it hot or cold there? Windy? Tropical? These are the sort of details which lift writing to higher levels.

Changing settings   A child's story may take place in multiple settings. As children move their story through time and space, it is important that they remember to include detail about the setting each time a new locale is introduced.

Props   These are a fun way to bring the setting to life. Simply refer to the everyday objects that characters encounter in a story's setting. Depending on the story, these might be gold coins or a tiara, a space ship or a teddy bear.

Tone and mood

Tone and mood are also influenced by a story's setting. Contemplate a story set during the summer on a cruise ship in the Caribbean versus a story set during a cold and bleak stormy winter at a remote farmhouse on the moors. Characters and events are affected by the setting in which they find themselves such as weather, temperature, lighting etc. These factors impact the mood and tone of a story. You can talk to children about this. A story can be 'happy' or 'sad', but it isn't just the plot which impacts this. The setting can as well. Once they recognise this, they can use this information to assist them as they create their own stories.

Whole Class
Exercise 3

Discuss in pairs how the Caribbean scene
makes the children feel. Then, as a class, complete a
shared write to describe the setting. It will evoke a positive,
happy mood and tone.

Now, repeat the process with the stormy-scene photograph on page 46. Note how setting can impact on the mood and tone. Explain to the children what mood and tone are.

Mood is when a writer evokes feelings in readers through the use of their words and description. Helping children to understand this gives them more command over the way in which they write. They will be more likely to make conscious decisions about their choice of words if they're bearing in mind the impact that they want to have on their readers. This is helping them to develop the skill to create a tone.

How to Achieve Outstanding Writers in the Early Years Foundation Stage and Key Stage 1

Setting Exercises

Fill in the gaps   Provide your class with some sentences which have words missing. Think of some words to fill in the gaps so that the sentence makes sense. Here is a (completed) example:

Lucy <u>bolted/swaggered/sat</u> down outside the <u>prison/aeroplane/café/</u> for breakfast. The welcoming smell of <u>bacon/rotting fish/drains</u> filled the air. While she sat drinking her coffee, she heard someone <u>laughing/crowing/shuffling</u> behind her. It was her <u>friend/donkey/ owner</u>, Maggie, who asked, <u>"Can I join you for breakfast?"</u>/ "Where's my onion?"/ "Do you want to buy a dragon?"

This is a great way of setting a scene really quickly and helping children to establish a setting for their writing. You can provide a list of words to choose from if it helps them. These exercises can turn out to be really funny, and children delight in reading out their results. After the exercise has been completed, ask children to expand on the opening paragraph and see if they can make it into a story.

Creating a setting   Ask children to create a setting with the word or caption provided. Remind them to use any, or all, of the five senses (see, hear, taste, smell, touch) to describe the setting. Here is an example to show the class:

'A bus'. The bus has blue seats and big windows. There are lots of red bells to push, in case you want to stop, which make a loud bleep! Someone is eating chips, and the whole place smells of vinegar! The back window is open and lets in the cold night air. The noise coming from the passengers talking is rather loud.

Now ask them to try it themselves, with the following phrases:

1. A dentist's surgery or office
2. A beach
3. A baker's shop
4. A barbecue

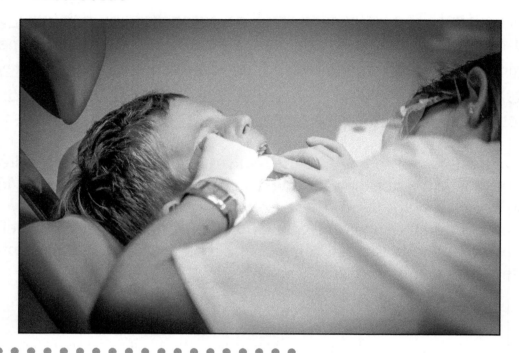

Five words   Read each scenario to your class and then, for each situation, come up with five words or phrases that you think of in reaction to the word. These can then be used to construct a setting. Here is an example to show the class:

Becky is having her 7th birthday party.

1. Saturday
2. Soft play
3. Shouting
4. Burgers
5. Milkshakes

It was Saturday morning, Becky was having a party – it was her 7th birthday! All her friends came to soft-play and it was noisy because everyone was shouting. She got lots of presents. They had burgers for lunch and the onions smelt so yummy. The milkshakes were vanilla and strawberry.

Now ask your class to try these independently:

Daniel is visiting his uncle:

1. _____

2. _____

3. _____

4. _____

5. _____

Toby is riding his bike:

1. _____

2. _____

3. _____

4. _____

5. _____

Design a sweet factory   Another firm favourite of the children's. Ask them to come up with a name for the factory and then write a description of it. What are the different rooms like? Use all the senses to describe it.

I usually go back to this activity the following day and ask children to imagine that they're taking a tour of the factory with their family. Using action and dialogue, try to reveal more of the setting. Example:

Bailey skipped through the 'squishy' room. She leapfrogged over the giant marshmallows and bounced on the jelly baby stepping stones. "Look out for the candy floss clouds," she called to her brother Seth.

More Setting Exercises

Invent a new place to go on holiday.
Write about it using all of your senses. Think of a name for your setting.
Don't forget to think about climate and weather. What time of year is it
there? Include all these details in the description.

You have found a mysterious key.

Explore your school, try to find the correct door that it opens. At the top of
a staircase, that you have never seen before, you see a door with a sign that
says 'Smile zone'. You open it up and cannot believe your eyes … . Write
about the smile zone and what happens on the other side of the door.

What is the first thing you think of when you hear or see the word ridiculous?
Write about a land that only has ridiculous laws.

Imagine that there is a new season. What is it called and what happens
during that season? What is the weather like? Does it have festivals? Tell us
all about it.

Imagine the world suddenly has no electricity anymore. Write about how
that changes your house and school.

You have been asked to design a new city. What will you call it? What sort
of buildings do you want to include? What about things like parks, schools
and hospitals? Write about what your city is like.

You are the president/leader of another planet. What is your planet like?
Talk about the geography and the climate. What else lives there?

Imagine you own a shop that only sells things which are purple. Describe
what your shop is like and the type of products that you sell.

Describe the house of 'The old woman who lived in a shoe'.

Describe the house of an old man who lived in an unusual place. Maybe it was a teapot or a pan. You decide. Tell us about it, using your senses.

Design your dream tree-house. Maybe it has a ball pen, a slide and a fireman's pole. Tell us about it using action and dialogue. Imagine you are up there, with your best friend.

What is your favourite month of the year? Write about why you like it and some of your favourite things to do during that month.

Magic-go-round. Every night at midnight, the carousel horses came to life and flew off to where? Describe the funfair, and then describe the place that the horse flies away to.

Pretend you have just woken up in a tent. You unzip the flap to find you are in the middle of a jungle. Describe the setting around you.

Imagine your house has been turned upside down. Write about your upside down house.

Describe what it would be like to be caught outside in a thunderstorm. Whereabouts are you? What does it feel like? Tell us using all your senses.

Pretend that you have found a time machine and have gone back to the 50s. What is our school like in that era?

Write about going for a walk in your local park. Write four paragraphs, one for each season. Think about how mood and tone changes according to the weather, climate and time of year.

Super city. Where is this?

Tribute? Where is this mysterious construction located and what is it used for?

Saamis Tepee, Medicine Hat Visitor Centre, Calgary, Canada.

Write a story about a family of badgers who live in the forest. What is their home (*sett*) like?

Plot

Storytelling includes many elements that a writer must bear in mind. Plot is foremost among these components. Plot is the order of events that make up a story. The plot is the story, and more precisely, how the story advances, unfolds and moves in time.

There are countless plot strategies that storytellers can utilise to improve the plotting procedure. It is helpful to introduce some of these basic plot elements that make for good storytelling to children.

Backstory

There's more to each story than what we actually read. Every character has a past and there are customarily essential events that have occurred preceding the story. This is backstory, which is what transpired before this story began. Although most backstory never seeps into the narrative, it's valuable for a writer to have an understanding of backstory, as the details of the past will trickle into the story and this makes writing richer and more realistic. Of course, children are not expected to conjure up a whole realm of backstory before they begin to write. But it is useful to bear this in mind and to give it some consideration when starting to create a story of their own.

Whole Class Exercise

Share a picture book with your class. Now put the children into pairs. Think about the opening scene and the main character. What do the children think are some of the things that occurred before this story began?

For example,
The Very Hungry Caterpillar begins with an egg on a leaf. Rewind a little. How did the egg get there?

Ask the children to think about it and then write the scene that occurred before the story starts.

The hook

A narrative hook is a literary method in the beginning of a story that 'grabs' the reader's interest so that they will continue reading. It's placed near the start of a story to lure readers to keep turning pages. Hooks frequently offer mysteries, or fascinating questions, and make the reader curious enough to want to find out what happens next. There are different types of hook.

The puzzle hook leaves the readers with more questions than answers. They want to know what, why, when, where and how?

The action hook launches into action immediately with no preamble, no scene-setting and no long descriptions. You need to catch up as you go along. What you get is that the story kick-starts from the word go.

The character hook can simply be a description of the character, what they're up to and who they are. The more interesting the character, the better.

The scenic hook is a similar approach, only this time the writer launches into an interesting description of the setting.

The dialogue/conversation hook begins the story with the interaction between characters which can compel readers to keep going.

All of these are valid ways to start a story. In making children aware of the different techniques, you are giving them more strings to add to their plotting bow.

The inciting incident

The inciting incident is the occurrence that launches the story. It is different to the story opening in that it is the event which 'gets things going'. In other words, something happens which the main character has to address. Most stories commence by showing us the main character in their 'ordinary world'. Next, something happens which pushes the protagonist onto some other path. Inciting incidents can be intertwined with a story's opening hook. The inciting incident in *The Three Little Pigs* is that each of the pigs obtains different building materials for their own house: straw, sticks and bricks.

Whole Class Exercise

Read Cinderella with your class. Can they identify the inciting incident? It's when the invitation to the ball arrives. Now, write a new story about the stepsisters and what happened to them after Cinderella got married. Come up with an inciting incident as a class and then ask the children to work in groups to create a new story. They can act it out for each other and then write it up.

Conflict

I have already covered this storytelling element in the character chapter. Some plot elements are non-compulsory. Conflict is not. Without conflict, there is no story. Characters want something they don't have, or they must defeat challenges which they have encountered.

Climax

Like conflict, climax is a necessity of storytelling. This is the moment when a story reaches its pinnacle.

How to plot

Plotting is reasonably demanding. It can be more difficult for some than others to generate plots that seem original. Tell children that often innovation comes not from plotting, but from generating distinctive and well-defined characters and blending assorted story components in different ways.

Everyone approaches fiction writing by means of whatever technique suits them best as an individual. There is no right or wrong way to go about this.

Plot planning

I usually ask children to think about their character and setting and make some notes about these. It can be helpful for some children to make a plot outline using time connectives:

First … Then … Next … And … Finally …

However, I'm an advocate for allowing children the freedom to sit, and simply let the writing flow, and see where it takes them. They will not always end up with a neat plot, but the more that they practise this, the better accomplished they will become at bringing together different elements.

Story mountain

Using a story mountain can help. These simply involve dissecting a familiar story, and adding key elements from the start at the foot of the mountain. The rising tension comes next. Then add the peak of the narrative at the crest of the mountain before putting the ending at the second foot of the mountain on the other side.

Whole Class
or Individual Exercises

Write a story starter for the photograph below which launches the narrative with a **puzzle hook**.

Whole Class or Individual Exercises

Write a story starter for the photograph below which launches the narrative with a **puzzle hook**.

How to Achieve Outstanding Writers in the Early Years Foundation Stage and Key Stage 1

Whole Class
or Individual Exercises

Write a story starter for the photograph below which launches the narrative with a **puzzle hook**.

Exercise

Write a story starter for the photograph below which launches the narrative with an **action hook**.

How to Achieve Outstanding Writers in the Early Years Foundation Stage and Key Stage 1

Exercise

Write a story starter for the photograph below which launches the narrative with an **action hook**.

Exercise

Write a story starter for the photograph below which launches the narrative with an **action hook**.

How to Achieve Outstanding Writers in the Early Years Foundation Stage and Key Stage 1

Exercise

Write a story starter for the photograph below which launches the narrative with a **conversation hook**.

Exercise

Write a story starter for the photograph below which launches the narrative with a **conversation hook**.

Exercise

Write a story starter for the photograph below which launches the narrative with a **conversation hook**.

Exercise

Write a story starter for the photograph below which launches the narrative with a **scenic hook.**

How to Achieve Outstanding Writers in the Early Years Foundation Stage and Key Stage 1

Exercise

Write a story starter for the photograph below which launches the narrative with a **scenic hook.**

Exercise

Write a story starter for the photograph below which launches the narrative with a **scenic hook.**

How to Achieve Outstanding Writers in the Early Years Foundation Stage and Key Stage 1

Exercise

Write a story starter for the photograph below which launches the narrative with a **character hook.**

Exercise

Write a story starter for the photograph below which launches the narrative with a **character hook.**

Exercise

Write a story starter for the photograph below which launches the narrative with a **character hook.**

Story Ideas Exercises

Have a look at these ideas as a class and discuss them. Then let the children have a go at plotting and writing a story from the prompts.

What if you got home to find an enormous box had been left in your front garden addressed to you? What on earth is inside when you open it and what happens next?

• •

Imagine that you woke up one day and you had grown a pair of wings overnight. Where is the first place that you would fly to and what would you do when you got there?

• •

You have been given the chance to either become invisible or have the power to read minds. Your sister or brother will get the power that you reject. Which do you choose and what happens next?

• •

You are walking through the woods when one of the trees begins talking to you. What does it say?

• •

It is national 'Kids are in charge day' and your Mum and Dad have to do everything you want. What are you going to do with your day and what happens next?

• •

You get to school to find that a UFO has landed in the playground, and they will only talk to a person who has your name. Will you go aboard the space ship and what do they say to you?

• •

Write a sequel to a popular fairy tale. What happened to Sleeping Beauty when she lived happily ever after? What does that mean exactly? Tell us about it.

• •

You wake up to discover that your whole house is now made out of food. Your bed is a giant doughnut and your stairs are made out of cookies. Everything is edible. Now what?

Narrative Point of View

If readers imagine the occurrences of a story as a film streaming in their minds, then the narrative point of view can be described as where the camera is positioned. The narrator of a story is the in-world storyteller, the voice that communicates the tale to the reader. Narrative point of view ascertains the perception of the narrator, relative to the story. Points of view can be first person, second person or third person.

In the case of first-person point of view, we see the story through their eyes. In limited third-person point of view, that character is not telling us the story, but we're attached to their outlook of happenings. In all-seeing third-person point of view, the narrator can describe everything in the story objectively.

First person

In a first-person narrative, the narrator is usually the main character. First-person point of view is easily identified by the narrator's use of 'I'. It is worth pointing out to the children that first-person narrative can also be relayed by a secondary character but this is less common.

The first-person point of view provides plentiful opportunities to present a narrator with a well-defined voice, which adds to the story's tone. First person habitually feels as if we're inside the narrator's mind and listening to their thoughts. It can make readers feel closer to a character as though they know them well. First-person narration can feel more personal, as if the reader is in a close discussion with the narrator.

Second person

Second-person narratives use the pronoun 'you' to refer to other characters or the reader. These stories are designed to make it feel as though the reader is the main character in the story. This point of view is rarely used in storytelling. It features in 'choose your own adventure' stories and also in video games. It is not usually a style that children will adopt when writing in school, but it is worth introducing them to in order to broaden their knowledge.

We tend to see second-person point of view used generally in instructions, for example, recipes or other written instructions such as how to put furniture together.

Third person

Third-person point of view is the most commonplace type of prose narrative because it presents the greatest flexibility with access to all characters and full view of the story world and all events taking place. Characters are referred to as he, she, and they.

A third-person omniscient narrative has absolute knowledge of the story and characters at all times. The narrator knows everything in the story world but may choose which details to reveal to the reader. A third-person limited narrative only has full knowledge of one character and can only communicate events that character is privy to.

Narrative point of view is a chief matter for writers because when creating a story, it shapes the distinct perspective from which readers observe the story events unfolding. People tend to prefer writing in either first or third person. I encourage children to try to alternate which they use.

Whole Class Exercise

Look at the picture below and prepare a description created from a third-person point of view.

Show the photograph to the class, reading them the description which you have already created. Now, as a class, write about what is happening from the surfer's point of view. Try to include detail using sensory descriptions. For instance, "The seawater tastes so salty and went into my eyes, and made them sting. The roar of the waves was so loud when the water came rushing towards me after I fell off my board." Compare the two different approaches. Now ask your class to do the same thing individually.

Points of View Exercise

Ask the children to think of a story that they know well and to write a version of it from another point of view. For instance, they could write *Cinderella* from the point of view of one of the ugly sisters or, perhaps, write *The Three Billy Goats Gruff* from the point of view of the troll.

Create a character who performs at a talent show audition. He thinks he is exceptionally good and that on the night everything went exceedingly well. However, the main judge who watched the performance thought it was terrible!

Write this scenario from both character's points of view.

Your character goes with a friend to buy a new outfit. Your friend tries on a hideous outfit. Your character pretends to love it. Your friend was only playing a joke by choosing to try on those clothes!

Write the scenario from both people's points of view.

Your friend borrows your bike without asking and dents the front wheel. How do you deal with it? Write the scene from both characters' points of view.

Which season do you like best: winter or summer? Write about the reasons why you think winter or summer is better. Then, write as though you actually prefer the other season the best!

Imagine you have invented a robot and you are teaching him how to do laundry, mix drinks and make sandwiches. Write the scene from both yours and the robot's points of view.

Show, Don't Tell

When you tell, rather than show, you basically provide your reader with information instead of permitting them to infer it. This is because you are providing details by simply asserting them. You may report that a character is 'irritated' or 'cold'. That's telling. Showing, however, paints a picture for the reader to envisage in their mind's eye. When you show, rather than tell, you involve the reader by making them a part of the experience.

When a writer 'tells' something to a reader, they're removing the prospect for them to discover, and get involved, by coming to their own conclusions. 'Telling' often keeps a reader on the outside of the story, instead of allowing them to become immersed. The reader doesn't want to be disclosed that the character is tired or happy. They want to feel it for themselves!

'Show' is a tool used to tug the reader to a narrative. In teaching children to use it at an early age, you are giving them the ability to create a connection between the reader and their story and characters. This transpires because they will be compelling the reader to figure out what's happening, instead of telling them what they should comprehend or feel. This is a way in which young writers can learn to keep the reader actively involved in the story.

Whole Class Exercise

Show the class the photograph below. Ask them how they
think the children in the picture are feeling. They will tell you that
they are scared. Now, ask the children to work in pairs to come up
with a description of the picture that tells what is happening and how
they are feeling without using the words 'scared', 'afraid', 'frightened' etc.

Dialogue

Having taught children that it is better to try to describe what is occurring rather than to just tell the reader, I then usually explain the exception to this rule and that is to use dialogue.

Dialogue is the most straightforward way of 'showing'. This is one way in which you can directly state how a character is feeling by directly naming an emotion. For example, in a description for the below picture, a writer could scribe; *Kim was sad.* This is not a powerful approach. However, should the writer put; *"I'm sad," said Kim as he stared tearfully at the floor.* This is a much more effective way to communicate the information and the fact that the character has stated the emotion makes it an acceptable way to show the feeling. Even better is to include the reason 'why' a character might be feeling a certain way; *"I'm sad," said Kim, "because so many people have died."*

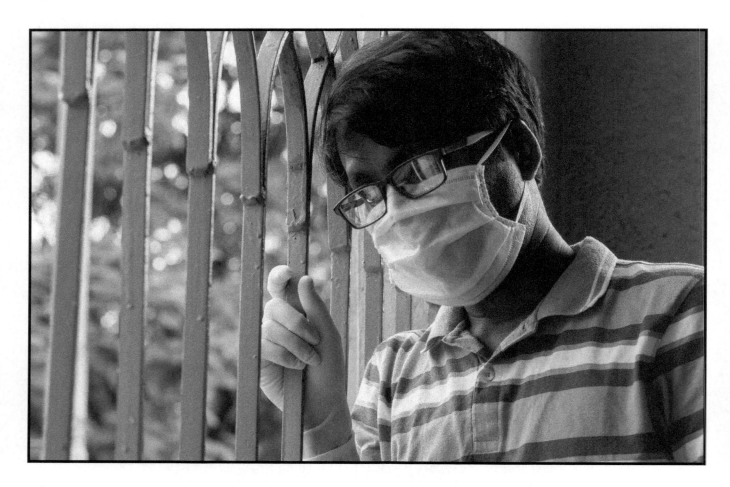

Of course, you don't want children to have characters state their every emotion as a story progresses, but this is a tool which can be utilised along with all the others in this book in moderation in a piece of work.

Actions and reactions

Remind children not to simply tell their readers about the temperament of their characters, instead show them through their actions. That will reveal the personality of the characters. How a character acts and reacts to the events in a story lets a reader know what this character is like as a person.Instead of saying, "He was a cruel person," describe a character kicking over a dog's water bowl, on a hot day, on purpose. In doing this, a writer immediately convinces the reader that the character is not a good person.

Look at the picture below. We immediately like the man in the photograph because of his actions. Ask your class to write a description about what is happening, and then come to a decision about the sort of person this man is. This will help them to understand that, just as we judge real-life people by their actions, so too do we judge characters in stories.

Whole Class Exercise

For each of the examples below, ask your class to write a
short description of the character doing something that will make the
reader like that person.

Now repeat the process, but this time have the character do something
which shows that they are not such a good person. This will help children
to practise communicating information about characters and show them
how they, as writers, can influence their readers.

1 – A bus driver

2 – A dragon

3 – A teacher

4 – A pirate

5 – An alien

Body language

Humans communicate a great deal in non-verbal ways. So, becoming skilled at including
descriptions of characters' body language, children will become proficient in the use of a
powerful tool at their disposal to aid them in showing, rather than telling. This involves including
details about body language and facial expressions.

As humans feel emotions, we react differently, in a physical way. For instance, when we are sad,
we often cry. When some people are angry they clench their fists. If excited, some people jump
up and down. We yawn when we are tired.

Whole Class Exercise

Call a child to the front of the class and whisper an emotion in their ear. Ask them to act it out and then see if the rest of the class can guess it. Now, all of you have a go at acting out that emotion. When you have done that, scribe all the different facial expressions, feelings and body language associated with that trait. When you have done this, create a 'body language/ facial expression' thesaurus. You can display this on the wall or make a whole class book but leave it available for children to refer to when they're completing their writing.

Show, Don't Tell Exercises

Sentence expansion   Ask your class to look at the following and rewrite them, so that they're 'showing' the reader what is happening instead of telling them.

1 – Sam was sleepy.

2 – It was winter.

3 – Kelly was a footballer.

Guess the secret   Put the children into pairs and give them a piece of paper with information about a made-up character. For instance, 'Jill does not like Jack' or 'Mary's lamb got lost'. Now, get them to write a paragraph about the information which they have been given, and read it out to the class. See if the class can guess the character's 'secret'.

Seeing red   Show the class the photograph of this man. Describe how someone's dialogue, body language and facial expressions change when they get angry. Discuss with the class, the types of situation that can cause people to become angry.

Action and Dialogue

You will already have discussed action and dialogue with your class, after working through the previous chapter. Action and dialogue are the motion that propel a story onward. When characters do things, that's action. When they talk, that's dialogue. Most of a story's thrust is comprised of action and dialogue.

Characters walk and talk. They run and jump and hide. They laugh and giggle and cry and do a thousand other things. They have discussions and arguments and joke with each other. That's what makes the story unfurl: through action and dialogue. So it is worthwhile exploring these concepts with your class in more detail.

Action

Action can be presented in different ways in a narrative. It can be encompassed within a sole word: escape. It can be an entire chapter that shows a character being chased, through a shopping mall, climbing onto the rooftop, before leaping onto a trailer of hay and burying deep down to hide, as the vehicle makes its way out of town, taking the character with it.

But action isn't always high drama. It is also about the routine every day, ordinary world around characters and the behaviours that they engage in it. This means that including some details about action can be a good way to add realism to a story, such as when characters eat and drink whilst engaging in a chat.

Everything that characters do is action. Having a cup of tea. Walking to the shops. Playing tag in the playground. Blinking their eyes because they got sand inside them when the wind blew. Writing about action helps a reader to get to know a character, and also helps to tell the story as it enables a plot to unwind.

Action often increases as the story moves towards the climax. The stakes get higher. Talk to children about this, and explain that this is called 'pacing'. For instance, if a character is being chased by pirates who are angry because he has stolen their treasure, it is hardly appropriate for the person being chased to sit down and have a cup of tea. Action tends to be more drawn out at the start and middle of a story, and faster and more intense towards the climax and ending.

Whole Class Exercise

Read some picture books and then, once you have done this, go through the story, and add sticky notes to mark where the key action takes place. Have one colour for 'low action', and another colour for 'high action'. Now put the children into pairs with their own picture book. Have them repeat the task to see if they're able to identify these independently.

Action Exercises

Some of these feature high action and some of them low action. The idea is to get children used to thinking about generating writing that describes characters involved in actively doing something. They can include dialogue, but encourage them to really focus on what characters are doing.

1. Aliens have kidnapped your brother, and his class, and imprisoned them in a warehouse. It's up to you, and your friends, to save the day. You find yourself outside the warehouse at midnight. How will you get inside to rescue your brother?

2. It is sports day, and you are about to participate in the 'egg and spoon race'. After that, you are going to complete the hurdles and then the 100 metres. Write a description in the first-person about the action that occurs.

3. You are in a hot air balloon that isn't supposed to fly away, but the rope breaks and you are floating off into the air … .

4. You are a racing car driver and about to participate in a big race with lots of spectators. Describe the race and what happens next.

5. Your mum has sent you to the shop to buy some milk. Write about the trip there and back and what happens to the milk when you get it home.

6. It's your birthday and you are having a party at the swimming pool. What happens when all your friends arrive?

7. Pretend that you are in the circus and you work as a tightrope walker. It is your turn to perform. Describe what your act involves.

8. Write about what your day would be like if you were a train driver.

9. You are in the school canteen about to get lunch, but they have run out of chips just as you get to the front of the line. What happens next?

10. Your character is on the run after being accused of stealing diamonds from a jewellery store. You are hiding in an abandoned barn, but now the police have arrived. What happens next?

Dialogue

Brilliant dialogue can elevate a story to new heights. Dialogue is an articulation of the characters that exposes their personalities and it can also be used to advance a plot. Well-crafted dialogue can intensify a reader's commitment with the characters, as well as the story.

Dialogue can also enhance characterisation by making characters distinct via the way in which they talk. Characters from one country will have distinct expressions and use of language, compared to characters from another country. This also applies to different areas, and regions, of the country. This is something that children love to explore.

Whole Class Exercise

Have a whole class discussion. Think about turns of phrase
and expressions that are unique to the area in which your school is
located. Write them down. Now pick another area. Look up some phrases
and expressions which are unique to that particular location. Compare them
to the list which you have already generated. There are many websites
which provide this sort of information and children find it fascinating.
Ask them to write some dialogue between two characters. One
from your own location and one who comes from
the area that you have researched.

As well as being influenced by the locale in which they live, people, and therefore characters, also have individual speech patterns, habits and quirks. Lots of people have a very distinct way of speaking. Generally, all of us have particular words that we frequently use or certain ways of threading words together that vary somewhat from our friends and family and those around us. For instance, perhaps there is someone you know who calls everyone "Darling" or somebody who starts every other sentence with the word "like ...". Dialogue that is shaped in a way that is distinctive to each character can add authenticity. Again, the key to doing this successfully in a story is to use this tactic sparingly. You do not want children to obsessively make a character use the word 'Awesome' every time they utter anything. But, if they repeat it two or three times whenever they're pleased by a turn of events, it will help to shape their personality and distinctiveness.

Dialogue Exercises

Below are some dialogue exercises. Give them to the children and ask them to just start writing a dialogue between two characters using the prompt as an opening line. They don't have to know who the characters are, where they are or why they're saying what they're saying. These exercises are just about letting children practise that art of creating dialogue.

1. "I thought you were going to make pizza for dinner."

2. "We are totally lost."

3. "I'm never going to wear a hat again."

4.   "Don't look at me like that."

5.   "How many balloons have we blown up now?"

6.   "Has anyone seen the remote control?"

7.   "How much longer till we're there?"

8.   "Let's just not say anything."

9.   "If you don't tell them, I will."

10.   "How many more times? I said, no!"

11.   "This is all your fault."

12.   "You are going to drop that if you aren't careful."

13.   "Your favourite TV show has just started."

14.   "Shall we go to the beach?"

15.   "I have something exciting to tell you."

16.   "Do you want to finish my sandwich?"

17.   "Quick! Come and look out of the window!"

18.   "I thought it was over and done with."

19.   "I don't want to go to bed."

20.   "Let's just throw it away."

Action and dialogue working together

Action and dialogue function best within a story when they work together and are intermingled in a flowing way. Characters, therefore, should do things while they converse. They eat and talk. They drive and talk. They walk and cook and talk. As well as this, they also use body language and make facial expressions. Dialogue and action are crucial to storytelling but, as with all elements of storytelling, both the action and the dialogue should be necessary to the story and should move it forward in meaningful ways.

Theme of a Story

Theme is the underlying message of a story. It is essentially a worldview, outlook, moral idea or ethical question. It is the topic at the centre of the story, or narrative, that the writer wants the reader to become aware of and consider as a result of reading the story. Theme can communicate an idea or notion to a reader about life or human nature. Many stories have more than one theme.

Themes are often universal in nature. Some frequent common themes in children's literature are courage, friendship, identity, family, loss, growing up and kindness. All children's stories contain an underlying theme and these are usually fairly easy to establish.

Of course, the theme of a story is never straightforward or simply told to the reader. The reader needs to come to their own conclusions after reading the story and then make an inference.

You can explain to the children that if you, as a teacher, put the kettle on and took out a mug, teaspoon and teabag that they could infer that you were about to make a cup of tea. They would be able to work that out by putting the information together. This is the same skill set that they have to use in order to consider a story's theme.

How to Achieve Outstanding Writers in the Early Years Foundation Stage and Key Stage 1

Whole Class Exercise

Explain to your class that the theme of a story will never be specified overtly and that, as readers, they will have to deduce and draw their own conclusions in order to recognise the theme of a story. Now, read the story *'Beauty and the Beast'*. Ask the children what they think the theme of the story is.

I'd say that the theme for *Beauty and the Beast* is that, being beautiful is not on the outside of a person but what lies on the inside. By this I maintain, that the behaviour of a person and his/her personality is far more important than their looks, like being kind, sensitive to the needs of others, willing to help those in need, etc. Someone else may identify a different theme. There is no right or wrong answer. It is left to the reader to make their own decision. Once I have covered the topic of theme with my class, I make it a habit to always ask them to discuss the underlying theme of a story every time we share a picture book together. This only takes a few minutes and enriches story time. It also enables them to be aware of the layers involved in creating a story.

Questions for children to consider when trying to identify the theme

There are numerous ways a reader can piece together the story's theme. The reader can consider these questions:

1. Do the characters learn anything throughout the story?

2. Do the characters change at all?

3. Do the characters have any beliefs about life or people in general?

4. Why do the characters act the way they do?

When children have become proficient at identifying themes in other works, they will begin to attempt, and then get better, at bringing themes into their own writing.

I always emphasise that if they do not know what a story's theme is, then not to worry about it. Themes often emerge through plot naturally. Choosing a theme is often done subconsciously.

Poetry

Today was good

Today was fun

Tomorrow is another one.

All children can recognise a poem when they read or hear one. However, it can be a little more difficult to define what a poem is. I talk to my class about this before introducing poetry for the first time in an English lesson because it makes an interesting starting point. Of course, there is always the misconception that poetry has to rhyme. However, through a rich approach to this area, children become aware that this is not the case and are able to produce many different varieties of poems of their own. I build up all poems that children write over the course of a year and create a 'poetry portfolio' for each child.

Poetry is a category of literature that endeavours to arouse a reader's imagination or emotions. The writer accomplishes this by meticulously selecting and assembling words and through use of language for its meaning, sound and rhythm. Some poems, such as nursery rhymes, are straightforward and amusing, but there are countless forms of poetry.

Whereas poetry is a requirement of the National Curriculum, it is an area which is not always embraced in an all-encompassing way. Bringing poetry into your practice has enormous benefits and there are many ways to easily incorporate it widely so that the potential is fully realised.

Benefits of poetry for children

- Poems that rhyme have numerous benefits for children's literacy progress. Rhyming language can assist children who are struggling with their reading. This is because rhymes demonstrate to children that words are constructed of syllables. This aids them to identify the identical sound in other words. It also helps children to improve their spelling. If a child can spell 'cat', for example, they're then able to spell 'mat'. If they can spell 'chin', then they're also able to spell 'thin', assuming that they're familiar with their digraphs.

- Poetry develops children's vocabulary. Poems frequently encompass words which children do not usually stumble upon. As a result of the form's concise, accessible nature, it is usually straightforward to children to decode the meaning of the word from the surrounding context. This is also beneficial because they can use this skill when reading longer texts.

- Poetry introduces children to lots of literary concepts, such as alliteration, metaphors and similes. These frequently appear in nursery rhymes and children's poems. Becoming familiar with these concepts means that children are then able to utilise them in their own writing.

- Children's poems are usually easy to learn off by heart. Memorising a poem aids children to internalise configurations of language. When children recite a poem, they not only discover how to enunciate, but they also learn how to pronounce previously unfamiliar words. This assists with children's independent reading and also builds their communication skills.

- Poems can help children with their personal and social development in that reading poetry can develop empathy, as well as recognition and understanding of emotions. Poems reflect many different types of emotion and stir up feelings in a reader. This can be created not just through word choice, but by the way in which a poem is read aloud.

- Poetry cultivates children's imagination. In creating their own poems, they're tapping into a way of expressing themselves in a whole different manner.

- Learning poems off by heart benefits children's cognitive development.

- It allows children to see the world from another person's different point of view and appreciate how different cultures and beliefs vary.

Learning and reciting poetry

I learn a new poem off by heart with my class every two weeks. I accomplish this by learning a few lines each day. It doesn't take more than a couple of minutes, and these then add up very quickly. I also send home the new poem to parents so that they're able to join in and work on it with their children to assist in them memorising the poem.

I use an assortment of diverse techniques to help the children to make the poems come alive. I find it really beneficial to watch videos of poets performing their own poems and all children enjoy these. However, I then like to show children a *rap* video and discuss how this art form is also a type of poetry that has emerged over the last century. This not only grabs children's attention and gets them excited about poetry and reciting, but it also demonstrates that there are many different ways to write, perform and create poems.

There is a great deal more to poetry than simply reciting words. Also important is how these are interpreted. I like to incorporate music and musical instruments. We also add actions or mime events. At times we create a dance to go with a poem. In enriching the recital process, and going very deep with this experience, children's perception of poetry is broadened and they're able to engage with the material on a deep level. We also discuss intonation and volume of our voices which we can vary. All of these make poetry more accessible to children.

Poetry slam

I like to host a poetry slam once every term in which the children perform their poems for parents. Not only is this something which all parents adore attending, but it can also be used as a fundraiser for the school. I generally ask parents to send in poems which they love and create a display in the hall for them to explore before the performance starts. In addition, I ask for parent volunteers to perform their own poems. This is usually taken up and children love seeing the adults reciting poems for them.

Different poetic techniques

Onomatopoeia

Onomatopoeia is when a word describes a sound and actually mimics the sound, eg, hoot or moo. Onomatopoeia occurs frequently in children's poetry. It is a perfect way for encouraging young children to think about objects, people, animals, birds etc and the sounds they make.

Children grasp this concept very quickly. Have a whole class brainstorm session and create a list of as many onomatopoeic words that they can think of. Then read some poems that feature onomatopoeia. Explain to children that onomatopoeia can be real words or made up ones.

Whole Class Exercise

Onomatopoeia 1

Get the children to walk around the classroom and find things that make a noise and then generate another list with all of these things.

For example: Scissors: snip

Tap: plop, drip

Kettle: gurgle

As a class, create a poem called 'Our classroom'. Use all the words that you have created. Make up some words of your own to describe the sounds of the children! Scribe the poem on the whiteboard. It will paint a very vivid picture. I normally type this up and display it on the classroom door.

Now, ask the children to go and work independently and create a second poem, this time called 'The playground'.

Whole Class Exercise

Onomatopoeia 2

Fireworks are a fantastic starting point to get children to create an onomatopoeia poem. Watch some videos of firework displays on the whiteboard. Generate a list of words through a class discussion. You will get words such as: pop, bang, boom, whizz, etc. I always encourage the children to create their own as well, which they love. Now ask the children to write their own onomatopoeia poem.

Alliteration

Alliteration is when words are used in close succession that share the same initial sound. Children enjoy listening for alliteration and it is easy for them to quickly get the hang of creating their own alliteration sentences or poems.

Whole Class Exercise

Alliteration

Peter Piper picked a peck of pickled peppers is a classic example of **alliteration**. Alliteration is a fun way to use language which is almost as popular with children as rhyme itself!

Work your way through the register. Create a line of alliteration for every child's name in the class and scribe them on the whiteboard. Now ask children to go and work independently and do the same thing, this time using the names of individuals in their own families.

Repeated words

Repetition is a frequent occurrence in children's poetry. Repeated words are pleasing to listen to and agreeable to the ear. Poems do not simply contain repeated sounds (alliteration), but frequently they also can contain repeated words. Here's a classic example:

> Whether the weather be fine,
> Or whether the weather be not,
> Whether the weather be cold,
> Or whether the weather be hot,
> We'll weather the weather
> Whatever the weather,
> Whether we like it or not!

In the poem above, the use of the word 'weather/whether' has two meanings. Repetition does not have to be as sophisticated as this. It can be simply a word which is used frequently in a poem. Furthermore, it can be a sentence or phrase which comes at the end of every verse. A poem might start each line with the same words or it might repeat a stanza several times to create a chorus or refrain.

The use of repetition can help to create rhythm and bring attention to an idea. Repetition, therefore, helps to gain a reader's attention to a thought or feeling, that the writer is trying to communicate or it can simply make the poem more memorable, fun or enjoyable.

Exercises to help children to include repetition in poems

The easiest way to include repetition in a poem is to repeat the first words of each line through most or all of the poem. For example, if a child was writing a poem about why they loved school, it might read 'I love school because … ' at the start of each line.

Ask children to write a poem called 'For my Birthday … ' They will start each line the same way: 'For my birthday I want … '.

After the class have done the exercise above, discuss with them that a repeated phrase in a poem does not need to be long and it can actually just be a few words. For instance 'I like … ' or 'Tuesdays are … .'

Ask your children to think of two words to start a sentence and scribe the sentence. Now complete a poem with every sentence starting with those two words.

Rhyme

Poetry doesn't have to rhyme, but many children's poems do. Most children are very easily able to identify words which sound the same. However, there are always some who struggle with this. To assist them, read poems out that are displayed on the whiteboard and highlight the rhyming words in a bright colour to draw attention to them as you read the poem. This will help them to focus on and listen out for lines that end in the same sound.

There are different ways to incorporate rhyme into a poem. I introduce children to these because they're more than able to grasp the ideas and it helps them when they attempt to structure their own poems.

I begin using rhyming couplets with infant classes, but children need a lot of practice with rhyming words. Nursery rhymes are a great place to start. I frequently begin by reciting a common nursery rhyme with the children and we then alter the last word of the first line. *Twinkle, Twinkle, Little Star* might become:

> *Twinkle, twinkle, little frog*
> *Why do you bark like a dog?*

It is valuable to brainstorm rhyming words with the children before you start:
for example: car, far, bar, star, jar

> *On the road was a broken car*
> *It would not be going very far*

Couplets

These feature two rhyming lines in a row, as in:

> *Humpty Dumpty sat on a wall.*
>
> *Humpty Dumpty had a great fall.*

or

> *All the king's horses and all the king's men,*
>
> *Couldn't put Humpty together again.*

Whole Class Exercise

Couplets

Read Humpty Dumpty. Now rewrite it as a class. For example:

> Humpty Dumpty sat on the taps.
> Humpty Dumpty fell through the gaps.
>
> As he fell through the gaps, we heard him complain.
> It's dingy and dark down here in the drain.

Now get your children into pairs and ask them to have a go at coming up with some couplets about Humpty Dumpty. I stress that it doesn't have to make sense. The skill we are practising here is placing rhyming words at the end of each pair of lines.

ABAB

Sometimes, every other line in a poem will rhyme. This rhyming pattern is called ABAB as in:

> *Cold and raw the north wind doth blow*
> *Bleak in the morning early,*
> *All the hills are covered with snow,*
> *And winters now come fairly.*

Whole Class Exercise

ABAB

Write an ABAB poem about the winter. For example:

The rain comes down and the wind does blow.
I want to run and hide.
There's lots of hail and lots of snow.
I want to stay inside.

Have your children work in pairs and have a go at writing a poem themselves in this style. It is more challenging than using couplets, but children will enjoy it and again, the poem does not have to make sense. This is all about helping children to become accustomed to rhyming patterns.

Pyramid poems

Easy poems like the 'pyramid poem' are an approach which makes the form very accessible whilst also teaching children about language.

The pyramid poem opens with one word on the top line, and it adds a word on each consecutive line, thus creating a pyramid shape with the layout of the words on the page. The poems do not have to rhyme, and there are no obligations with regards to syllables or rhythmic patterns.

Pyramid poems involve writers describing a selected topic using one adjective in the second line, then two adjectives in the third line and so on. The children can add as many lines as they wish, with a short sentence at the end to round off the poem.

Here is an example:
> *Dolphin*
> *Laughing dolphin*
> *Laughing silver dolphin*
> *Laughing silver dolphin leaps*
> *Laughing silver dolphin leaps joyously.*

Topics for pyramid poems do not have to be complicated. They can be as simple as toys or cats. I typically link them to recent topics that we have covered in the classroom.

Before fabricating their own individual pyramid poems, I sometimes brainstorm a list of related vocabulary, as a whole class activity with the children.

A pyramid poem could have a distinct construction focusing on parts of speech.

- The first line is a single word, a noun.
- The second line includes the same noun and an adjective.
- The third line adds a verb.
- The fourth line adds an adverb.
- The fifth line includes all those words and a prepositional phrase.

I usually provide a handout sheet, which has been constructed in the shape of a pyramid, so that children simply have to add their words and the shape of the poem has been taken care of for them. I then ask them to draw an illustration underneath and then I display their work.

Acrostics

In an acrostic poem, the first letter of each line spells a word. The word is the topic of the poem and this word is usually also the title. Each line of the poem starts with the relevant letter in the topic word.

I usually start children off by asking them to write a poem about themselves using their name as the word which runs down the left-hand side of the page. As you can imagine, this is a very popular task. Here is an example:

<u>SETH</u>

<u>S</u>ometimes I like to play on my iPad.

<u>E</u>veryone thinks I'm great.

<u>T</u>hings I like are chips and pizza.

<u>H</u>ave you seen me play football?

Alphabet poems

There are various ways to approach these sorts of poems. None of these structures are required to rhyme. These poems feature alliteration, but are classed as a style of poetry in their own right.

The first method involves choosing a topic. For instance: The zoo. Now construct a sentence for each letter of the alphabet to feature in that is linked to the topic:

Alligators asked for apples.

Baboons borrowed a big ball.

Cockatoos called out for Coca Cola.

Another approach is to choose a theme, and link it to each of the letters in the following way:

A is for Apple

B is for Banana and Blackberries

C is for Cherries

Free poems

It's really important that children remember that poems don't always have to rhyme in order to be a poem. Similarly, we don't always have to tell children to write a poem for them to express themselves poetically.

Free verse is a literary tool. It can be explained as poetry that is free from restrictions of rhythm and does not rhyme. Although free poems don't make use of rhythm, rhyme schemes or other poetic methods, they still provide artistic expression and are equally valid.

Free verse is one of the easiest types of poetry to write because it is free from constrictions. However, this, in turn, can make it more difficult to approach because there is not a starting point or structure to adhere to. The writer has to work hard to create a piece of writing that is meaningful to them, without having any guidelines to follow.

The best way to encourage children to do this is to show them an image, and then give them some time to write freely about what they're feeling. Encourage children to choose their words carefully and think about the emotion, or feeling or topic, that they're trying to convey to a reader.

Sensory poems

A sensory poem is one that uses all five senses to describe something. These are common poems for primary school children. They're not problematic to tackle. There are a variety of ways in which to approach writing a sensory poem.

Whole Class Exercise

Sensory Poem

Write the five senses on the whiteboard and consider them with the class. Explain and discuss each sense. Now look at the photograph below and, as a class, answer the following questions, and create a sentence to describe the answer.

<u>Smell</u> – What can we smell?

<u>Taste</u> – What can we taste?

<u>Touch</u> – What can we feel?

<u>Sight</u> – What can we see?

<u>Sound</u> – What can we hear?

Tug of War Poem

We <u>smell</u> the grass.

We <u>taste</u> the excitement in the air.

We <u>feel</u> the rough rope.

We <u>see</u> the other team.

We <u>hear</u> the cheers around us.

Whole Class Exercise

First-person Sensory Poem

Ask the children to write a first-person sensory poem
about what they themselves would experience if they were in
the following picture.

How to Achieve Outstanding Writers in the Early Years Foundation Stage and Key Stage 1

Seven line sensory poem

This is related to a sensory poem, but it isn't written from the first person's point of view. It is structured as so:

1. Subject .... Train

2. Something you see .... Passengers everywhere

3. Something you smell .... Someone is drinking coffee

4. Something you hear .... Tickets, please!

5. Something you taste .... Toffee in my mouth

6. Something you touch/feel .... Holding my mum's hand tight

7. Repeat subject .... Train

Whole class exercise

Seven-line Sensory Poem writing

Ask the children to write a seven-line sensory poem about what they themselves would experience if they were in the following picture.

Nonsense poetry

Nonsense poetry is deep-rooted in language, and many of these types of poems have been passed down from generation to generation in the custom of oral folk tradition. Nonsense rhymes are playful, and illogical, and are designed to appeal to children. They're designed to evoke hilarity with their absurdity, and also cause bafflement in the reader. The secret behind nonsense poetry is that the verse is compiled principally of words entirely made up by the writer.

Nonsense verse is created to amuse by its inherent silliness. Tell the children not to worry about the results, and to just write freely. Let the children read their work aloud to each other. They're certain to laugh and giggle which means they have succeeded in their task.

Eletelephony

Once there was an elephant,
Who tried to use the telephant.
No! No! I mean an elephone
Who tried to use the telephone.

(Dear me! I am not certain quite
That even now I've got it right.)
Howe'er it was, he got his trunk
Entangled in the telephunk.

The more he tried to get it free,
The louder buzzed the telephee.
(I fear I'd better drop the song
Of elephop and telephong!)

Laura Elizabeth Richards (1850–1943)

"No mention of poetry would be complete without a nod to one of the most popular forms of all; the limmerick! Loved by children and adults alike. Edward Lear was a master of the limerick. He has hundreds to choose from. Here is one:

There was a young person in green,

Who seldom was fit to be seen;

She wore a long shawl,

Over bonnet and all,

Which enveloped that person in green.

How to Achieve Outstanding Writers in the Early Years Foundation Stage and Key Stage 1

Whole Class Exercise

Nonsense Verse

Ask your class to write a nonsense poem about the photograph below. Tell the children to feel free to fabricate as many new words as they desire to stand in place of nouns, verbs, adjectives etc.

Whole Class Exercise

Nonsense Verse

Ask your class to write a nonsense poem about the photograph below. Tell the children to feel free to fabricate as many new words as they desire to stand in place of nouns, verbs, adjectives etc.

More fun examples of nonesense poetry can be found in ...
Silly Verse for Kids by Spike Milligan
The Complete Nonsense of Edward Lear by Edward Lear
The Jabbawocky by Lewis Carroll.

Promoting poetry at home

Here are some ideas to send home for parents to get involved in promoting poetry:

1. Practise rhyming all the time when you are out and about, walking to school or in the car. Ask your child to think of rhymes for things you see around you.

2. Say a phrase to your child, and have them respond with a rhyming phrase.

3. Open a book to a random page and point to a word. Then ask your child to describe the images and thoughts that come into their head when they read it out loud.

4. Scribe single words onto scraps of paper to create free verse poems. Take it in turns picking a word to add to a poem.

How to create a poetry ambience in your classroom

Exhibit rhymes and poems around the classroom and school. Be imaginative. Display them on the back of doors, on noticeboards or over the sink. But go one step further. Laminate some poems and stick them onto plastic beakers the children use to drink from – and on the backs of their chairs!

● Include a poem in all assemblies.

● Create a 'poetry tree. It should have different branches according to the style of poem. Children can write poems on leaf-shaped paper to add to the tree. They can do these at home as well.

● Poetry basket. Have this in the reading area or on the carpet that children can dip into whenever they have a spare minute.

● Poem swap. Ask children to bring in a poem from home. Put them all in a box and then each child pulls out a new one and takes it home for a week. Repeat the process the following week, so they get a new poem every week.

Poetry prompts

You can link these to any of the poetry forms described above:

1. Write a 'recipe' for a dream. When they're all finished you can make a dream recipe book.

2. Write a poem using these five words: piano, cabbage, octopus, television, coat.

3. Imagine you shrank to the size of a mouse. What happens next?

4. Write an acrostic poem for the word 'celebration'.

5. Write a poem that starts with the word 'If'. (I usually read them the famous poem *If—*, Rudyard Kipling, beforehand.

Non-fiction

Non-fiction is any sort of writing that is centred on facts and real life, as opposed to a fictional story or poetry. There is a wide range of non-fiction texts. Non-fiction texts covered at primary school include: journalistic writing, instruction texts, recounts, information pieces, explanation articles, biography, argument and persuasive texts.

There is a whole array of things to incorporate here from writing informative texts, titles, contents pages, blurbs, instructions, captions, reviews and many more.

The first place to start is to ensure that children in your class are exposed to a wide range of non-fiction for them to read. This doesn't just include books, although these should be wide ranging and appealing and be widely available, not only in the book corner, but also in the independent books that they take home. Non-fiction books present children with the opportunity to learn about new notions and vocabulary. They can help to broaden their view of the world and teach about other cultures. They also nurture critical thinking and information-gathering capabilities. Good non-fiction makes those real-world associations which help children to grow and learn.

A lot of children really like to read about real people, places and events as well as learning about science, nature and the world around them through reading about it. Non-fiction books present information in appealing and thought-provoking ways for children. High-quality non-fiction encompasses the quintessence of life and provides details about who we are, information about the planet on which we live and the past, present and possible future. It explains how the world works.

Integrate non-fiction books into classroom areas. For example, put books about artists in the art area. Place books about architecture in the construction area. This not only exposes children to information texts, but also helps them to make connections and associations with the world around them.

As well as a wide-ranging collection of non-fiction books, there are other ways to expose children to this genre. Cut out interesting newspaper articles and mount them on cardboard and leave around the classroom for children to engage with. Bring in recipe books and instruction manuals. Atlases are also always popular. Travel brochures, programmes from shows and catalogues are also great.

Make sure you frequently explore non-fiction websites on the whiteboard with your class. National Geographic is fantastic. There are also many history websites. These are too numerous to list, but a simple Internet search will reveal them.

Whole Class Exercise

Non-fiction Book

I find it is beneficial to actively teach children how to navigate all the segments of a non-fiction book. Explain that the book will be organised around a specific topic or idea and we may learn new facts through reading it. Look at a non-fiction book as a class and point out the main features: table of contents, diagrams, captions, glossary and index.

Set the children into groups and leave a pile of books on their tables. Ask them to sort the books into two piles: fiction and non-fiction.

Pick a topic. 'Our School' is usually a good one. Now ask children to complete their own non-fiction book using the layout which they have been learning about. This will need to be completed over the course of a week as it is a big task, but children really enjoy participating in the activity. Because the writing is non-fiction, I tend to take photographs and print them out for the children to use in their books rather than having them draw illustrations.

How to get parents involved

1. Ask them to research places that they plan to visit with their children before they go. If they're going on holiday to Spain, why not research the area online before they fly out? This will not only expose their child to non-fiction texts through websites and possible travel books, but it will also build anticipation for their trip. It doesn't just need to be holiday destinations. It can be a trip to the theatre or cinema or even to the fish and chip shop. Why do we have fish and chip shops? Research it online and read about it!

2. Debate together! After parents have read an information book with their child encourage them to share their thoughts. What did they like or dislike about it? Is there something they want to learn more about that wasn't included in the book? How can they obtain that information? Library, Internet, etc. Non-fiction books for children often provide supplementary information for the adult on a page at the end of the book. These background notes can better aid adults to answer children's queries and start a follow-on discussion about the book.

Types of non-fiction writing

Every time I produce a classroom diagram or table with my class, I point out to them that we have created an informational, non-fiction piece of work. Over the course of the year, aim to introduce children to the concepts of a wide array of non-fiction writing. The variety and scope is very large, so there are plenty of opportunities to embrace this aspect of English wholeheartedly and enthusiastically.

Instruction texts

These sorts of non-fiction texts include things such as a recipe or manual. They usually feature a list of essential items which will be needed to complete a task. This is then followed by numbered directions on how to complete a certain activity. Instruction texts also frequently feature time connectives at the beginning of each numbered point ('First', 'Next', 'Then' and 'Lastly').

Have a wide range of instruction texts, such as recipes, manuals and game instructions in the classroom. These are easy to obtain. Parents are usually willing to bring in instructions that they no longer need, such as *How to set up your new mobile phone*, etc.

Whole Class Exercise

Instructional Non-fiction Activity 1

Write some instructions on the board for
how to play a game. I normally use *Snakes and Ladders*. Now
sit in a circle and play the game with a select number of children,
demonstrating that you are following the given instructions step by step.

For instance:

1) Firstly, give out the playing pieces.

2) Next, player 1 shakes the die and moves the counter according
to the number shown on the die.

If a player's counter lands on a ladder, then the player moves their
counter up to the square at the top of the ladder.

If the player lands on a snake, then the player moves their counter
down to the square at the snake's tail.

3) Then, player 2 repeats the process and so on.

4) Finally, the first player to the land at the finish, is the winner.

Discuss with your class the features of instruction texts. Next put
the children into groups and send them to their tables. Have a
different board game on each table along with some printed
out step-by-step instructions. Ask the children to read the
instructions and start to play the game. Depending
on reading ability levels, you may need
to scaffold with an adult in some
of the groups.

Feedback as a class about how easy it was to follow the instructions.

Follow up this activity the next day by having the children work in groups to create their own
board game. See next page for activity.

Whole Class Exercise

Instructional Non-fiction Activity 2

Display the step-by-step instructions used for *Snakes and Ladders*, played the previous day.

Ask the children to design and create their own board game. Let them individually draft and write the instructions about how to play their game following the example given in the *Snakes and Ladders* text. Then ask them to edit and improve their writing. Have they overlooked any of the main features? Do all their instructions make sense? Remind the children that the intention of an instruction text is to be clear and brief, as opposed to being descriptive. After they have finished designing their games and writing, let the children have an afternoon in which they rotate around the tables playing each other's games, trying to follow the instructions. They will adore doing this.

Other activities that can lead to writing instructional texts

Making puppets Hand puppets, string puppets, finger puppets – children love them all. Let them make their own and then write the instructions about how they did it.

How to be a good friend Pair the children up for the day with a buddy that they would not usually play with. Ask them to brainstorm things that make a good friend and then write a set of instructions to go along with these ideas. Make them into a book.

How to line up! Not the most exciting, but really effective! If you get tired of having to reinforce class rules, such as not cutting in line or pushing others out of the way, where to start the line and no talking etc, get the class to write up the instructions about how they should be doing it. It also works for tasks such as 'How to put on your coat!' (Don't forget to zip it up and use the hood in winter etc).

Papier mâché planets Or papier mâché anything really. Make the craft and then write the instructions about how you did it.

Clay finger pots These are always really popular.

The options are endless. You can tailor the activities and opportunities for writing instructions according to what is going on in your own classroom and around school.

Recount texts

A recount text is a type of writing that explains an event that has occurred. Some examples of these are diary entries or newspaper articles as well as letters. Recounts usually are written in the past tense and include the use of time connectives. These sorts of texts are usually written in chronological order and in the first-person tense.

Whole Class Exercise

Recount Writing

As a starting point, I usually share a diary entry on the whiteboard with the children about something that we have done as a class the previous day. For instance:

<u>First</u>, we went into the garden and pulled up all the weeds.
<u>Then</u>, we dug some holes and planted the seed potatoes.
<u>Next</u>, we covered them over with soil.
<u>Then</u>, we watered them.
<u>Finally</u>, we put our tools away.

I follow this up by asking children to work in pairs and tell each other what they did after school the previous day. Then ask them to write a recount about this individually.

Every time a memorable or exciting event occurs throughout the school year, ask the children to write a recount afterwards. I always follow up any school trip with a recount exercise. They're a good way to begin a new term as well because children can recount what they got up to in their school holidays. Other significant events might include visitors to the school, sports day, summer fairs etc.

Newspaper articles are also a fun way to approach this. The information provided is the same but it is given in a different format and widens children's exposure to the genre.

Information texts/non-chronological reports

An information text is one which provides information about a particular subject for example: space, elephants or football. Information texts are also known as non-chronological reports. This is because they report facts and information about a subject without referring to any particular order in which something has occurred.

Termly topics lend themselves well to non-chronological report writing tasks. No matter what your termly topic is, there is a way to find an excuse to complete some information writing. Obviously, some topics are designed for research and non-fiction writing: animals, for instance, or travel. With a topic such as fairy tales, there are still ways to incorporate non-fiction aspects. Why not research the *Brothers Grimm* or the origins of the countries in which fairy tales emerged? Did you read *The Little Mermaid*? Mermaids are not real but manatees are. This is the creature that sailors long ago mistook for mermaids. There are always opportunities for linking the area that you are exploring to a non-chronological report.

Things to consider when discussing how to write an information text are:
- main title
- sub-headings
- bullet points
- paragraphs
- pictures and captions

I find that it is helpful to carry out a shared write around research that, as a class, we have gathered on a topic. After this, ask the children to write up their own individual reports.

How to get parents involved
Ask them to carry out research at home on a topic that their child is particularly interested in and for them to create an information text about it. When they have done this, let the child read it out for the class and send them to the Head Teacher for a sticker!

Persuasive texts
Persuasive texts surround us in many ways. Children see countless examples of these in the world around them in the form of advertisements. For instance, adverts trying to encourage people to exercise more or adverts trying to entice people to buy a brand of cereal. These appear in the form of posters, on the side of buses, online, in newspapers and countless other places.

A good way to introduce children to this is to have an 'Enterprise week' when every class in the school makes something to sell. Have your class create posters for the item which they have made. Maybe they baked biscuits. Get them to write a poster to persuade other children in school why they should purchase them.

Non-fiction Exercises

Non-fiction Writing

Here is a selection of non-fiction writing prompts. Non-fiction writing prompts don't always have to be serious and sensible. There is no reason why you cannot be as creative as when setting tasks for poetry and story exercises. Below is a mixture of serious and less serious approaches to setting non-fiction writing tasks.

Ask parents to send in some photos of their children. Tell the children to write a recount of their memories associated with what is occurring in the photograph.

• •

Ask the children to plan their class end of term party. Write some instructions about how to decorate the room in preparation.

• •

Ask the children to share their memories about the last time they had their favourite food. Write a recount about this. Also, write an information text about how to prepare or purchase the food.

• •

Ask children to write instructions about how not to get wet in a rainstorm.

• •

Write a letter to your local MP.

• •

Write a letter to your class's favourite author.

• •

Write a letter to your local retirement home and send pictures as well.

• •

Write a letter to the Queen!

• •

Have the children interview each other and then write the results.

• •

Have the children interview their parents and write the results.

• •

An information text about why it is important to go to bed early.

• •

Instructions on how to build a house out of plastic bricks.

Instructions on how to play traditional playground games.

Instructions on how to decorate a Christmas tree.

Reasons not to be scared of the dark.

A non-chronological report about the history of your school.

What to do if you get lost in the supermarket.

An information text about how to clean your teeth properly.

Have the children try to interview their pets and write a newspaper article about the results.

Instructions on how to make someone laugh.

A recount about the last time you went to the cinema.

Write about your favourite smell, sight, taste, thing to touch and hear.

Your favourite way to spend a day.

Your favourite clothes.

What is a good alternative to playing tag?

How to make a kite.

Who is the greatest band in the world and why?

How to look after your teddy bear.

Meeting someone significant. How did you meet your best friend? Write a recount.

Create a timeline of events depicting your life by using newspaper headlines. Try to focus on events that didn't involve you directly, but connect them to the pivotal events in your life.

Take a boring event that happened today and write as much as you can about it.

Teaching Grammar: Tips and Ideas

Grammar is grasping how the portions of a sentence combine and how sentences are connected to one another.

The obvious starting point is using a capital letter and finger space. The other four main areas which are covered in Year 1 and Year 2 are nouns, verbs, adverbs and adjectives.

Nouns

A noun is a naming word. It is a thing, a person, an animal or a place.

A proper noun is the name of a person or place, such as Leila or London. Proper nouns start with a capital letter.

A common noun refers to a group of objects and does not have a capital letter, for example: hat, house or star.

A concrete noun is a person, place or object you can actually physically touch, such as: Mum, chair or water. Concrete nouns comprise both proper nouns and common nouns.

An abstract noun is something you cannot physically touch or see, such as love, happiness or fun.

Nouns are the building blocks of language and therefore writing.

In KS1, children are taught that nouns representative of people and places (proper nouns) begin with a capital letter. They're also taught to start replacing their nouns with pronouns and use the plural form of nouns, simply by adding 's' or 'es' to a word.

They may also learn about collective nouns and how to form nouns by using suffixes and a variety of prefixes.

Noun games

Noun treasure hunt Put the children into pairs to look for as many examples of concrete nouns as possible. They can do this in the classroom or any other location around the school. Set a time limit. The pair which gathers the most wins. Ask them to write their nouns (objects collected) and then put them into a sentence. Another variation of this is to find hidden sentences and then highlight the nouns when reading them out loud.

Stand up sit down Two children stand opposite each other. One child is asked to name a noun and the other then responds by saying an adjective. The reply has to be an adjective that goes with that noun, for example, bed and cosy. The game continues until either child loses.

Hot potato nouns Ask your class to stand in a circle. Throw a blow-up ball to a child and tell them they have ten seconds to think of a noun related to a topic you choose, maybe animals. The first child may say dog and then throws the ball to the next child who says mouse and so on.

Nouns all around Prepare a pile of alphabet flashcards and another set of cards with the words: person, place, thing, and idea on them. Choose two children and show them one of the cards from each pile. For example, 'B' and 'place'. A child might say 'Barbados'.

Packing nouns "I'm going on holiday and I'm taking _____." The noun must start with the letter A. The next child repeats the sentence but uses a noun that starts with the letter B and so on.

One minute list Give children a print out sheet with four columns, labelled: Person, Place, Thing and Idea. Children have a minute for each column to write down as many nouns as they can think of.

Flick to a page Children are all given a book from the reading area. Shout "Go". Children open the book to a random page and have to name a noun in the picture.

Name the activity Children have to list all objects needed to complete an activity and their classmates have to guess what it is. For example: goggles, towel, trunks – this would be swimming.

Adjectives

Adjectives are the words writers select to describe and give more detail. Children are encouraged to include adjectives in their writing to make it more descriptive and expressive. Children can at times rush forward with the action of a story, and may need to be reminded to slow down and consider the appearance of a character or setting. Using adjectives helps them to achieve this.

Using adjectives is a skill and selecting the right one to use in their writing is also important. Encourage children to be creative in their use of words. So instead of writing *sad*, they could write *miserable* or *distressed* or *heartbroken*.

How to assist children to include adjectives in their writing

☐ Provide a word bank of adjectives for children to access.

☐ Highlight nouns when marking a child's writing to prompt them to add an adjective to the noun. If time permits, ask them to rewrite a sentence to include an adjective.

- ☐ Complete shared writes on the Interactive Whiteboard to model how to feature adjectives within writing.

- ☐ Provide a thesaurus. Even better – make your own class thesaurus.

- ☐ Have a list of adjectives on display and build this up as the year goes on.

Adjective games

People bingo Provide children with an empty bingo board and some newspapers, comics and magazines. Children cut pictures of people out and glue them onto their bingo boards. Now call out different adjectives that can depict people: 'curly hair' or 'blue eyes'. If a picture on their board matches that description, they can cover the square. You can also make this game using photographs of children in your class.

Adjective elimination Show your class a picture. They have a minute to scribe as many adjectives to describe the picture as they can come up with onto their individual whiteboards. At the end of the minute, create a list on the main board of all the adjectives that have been generated.

Adjectives of a colour Collect paint sample cards which feature different shades of the same colour. Then provide children with two adjectives which have a similar meaning but different intensity. For example, annoyed/furious. Scribe the general adjective on the paler side of the paint sample and the more forceful adjective on the darker portion of the card. Then ask children to make their own set of cards with more pairs of adjectives.

Adjective dominoes You can then play a game of dominoes with the cards that you created in the previous exercise.

Growing sentences Scribe a basic sentence on the board. For example, *The girl is eating a sandwich*. Challenge children to add adjectives to the sentence. This works best by having them use their individual whiteboards.

Pair up game Ask children to write down a noun and an adjective on two small bits of paper. Ask them to walk around the room and see what other children have written. Join together as a class on the carpet. Make a list of all the nouns and adjectives that have been generated. Work together to match nouns and adjectives together and then create a sentence from them when they're matched. This is a really simple but effective game and produces some really fun and amusing sentences.

Verbs

Verbs are everywhere and children use them all the time in their writing. A verb is simply a doing or action word.

There are three main tenses which tell us when an action took place: present, past and future. Children need to decide whether they're writing in the past or present tense and ensure that the tense is kept consistent throughout. Children absorb a great deal with regards to verb tenses through listening, speaking and reading.

Verb Games

Charades Whisper a verb into a child's ear and then give them a time limit to mime it for their classmates. To embed the concept of verbs, I usually ask children to use the following phrase when they're guessing. For instance, the verb *run* would be guessed with "Are you running?"

Mother, may I ... Children stand in a line, and request permission to move forward by using the phrase "Mother, may I ... " For instance, "Mother, may I hop?" The person at the front responds, "Yes, you may" and this allows the children to move forward one step. "May I jump 3 times?" "Mother, may I walk 3 big steps forward?"

Twenty questions A child comes to the front of the class and is given a verb. The rest of your class are told to guess what the child's verb is by asking simple yes or no questions. For example: "Do you do it in the kitchen?" – "Yes."; "Do you do it with a knife and fork?" – "Yes."; "Is it eating?" – "Yes!"

Verb ball Children stand in a circle evenly spaced out. One child starts with a ball and throws it to the next child in line. The child catching the ball shouts an instruction for the group to follow, for example, "Everyone <u>jump</u>!", so all the children do that. The child with the ball then throws it on to the next child who then suggests a different action upon catching the ball.

Adverbs

Adverbs provide readers with information about a verb, explaining how, when, where or why an action is taking place. An adverb modifies a verb, which means that it tells a reader how, when, where or why something is being done. Adverbs usually end in *-ly*, but there are lots of exceptions.

When modelling writing on the board, ask children to suggest ideas for adverbs to add to a particular sentence. This is a kind of brainstorming that allows children to share ideas with each other and improve writing through a collaborative input and it also keeps them involved.

Underline verbs in a child's writing and ask them to add an adverb to their verbs. If there is time, ask them to rewrite the sentence.

Writing and Word Games

Here are a few more games which you can play whenever you have a spare 10 minutes or so in the classroom.

Consequences

Children love this game and it is really easy to organise. Get the class into groups of six. Ask the first child to scribe the name of a male, onto a sheet of paper and then fold the paper over so that the name is hidden. The second child has to write the name of a female and then fold it again, to conceal it. The third child has to write about where the two characters met. The fourth child has to write about what the male character said. The fifth child writes about what the female character said. The last child writes about something that happens at the end. Unfold all the papers and read them out for some funny stories.

Vocabulary grower

Introduce your class to a new word. I try to make it something really fun to say like 'haberdashery'. Explain what the word is and then ask the children to scribe a sentence using the new word. Now write a letter to someone in the room using the new word. This can be as silly as they like, in fact, the sillier, the better. Get them to swap letters with each other and read them out.

Crosswords

Crosswords are wonderful to help children learn new words and definitions.

Wordsearches

Most wordsearches are easy enough for children. They're a great way to get used to letter patterns and to improve spelling.

Scrabble

You can make your own bank of letters and laminate them and then play in groups of six. I like to make big boards out of cardboard sheets and let the children play on the floor or in the playground.

Free-writing Exercises for Children in Years 1–2

Here is a collection of some creative writing prompts and free-writing exercises and ideas to bring writing activities into your classroom.

Class mascot activity

Select a small soft toy which will become the class mascot. I like to take the class on a trip to a store to purchase the mascot because it makes it more special for the children and also helps them to invest in the toy. You could go to a specialist shop where you can stuff your own bear, a regular toy shop, market or even a local budget shop.

Once you have acquired the toy, choose a name for your mascot. You can make this into a writing exercise in its own right. Brainstorm a list of name ideas and then look up the meaning of the names by doing some research with your class using appropriate websites. As you are doing that, check the meaning of the children's names as well. For instance, the name Henry means: home, rich and ruler. Once the children are acquainted with their name meaning, they can write a character study based on a character who shares their name and possesses the traits linked to their name meaning. I have often asked children to create a story around this theme, and it has always been a successful and popular activity.

With your class, imagine a background for your new mascot. Where did the mascot come from before s/he went to the store? Write a character study about the mascot by doing a shared write. Then print it out and put it at the front of a 'diary'.

This diary will then be sent home with every child along with the mascot for one week at a time. During this time, encourage the children to keep a written journal of activities that the mascot has got up to whilst spending time with them and their family. The children can include photographs and drawings, along with their writing. The events do not have to be real. They can imagine that the mascot went into space or won the lottery if they so desire.

At the end of the year when the class move up to a new year group, send the mascot and the diary with them and ideally let it travel with them as they move through each year group.

Opening lines

Sometimes starting a story can be difficult and a blank page can lead to writer's block. Keep a container or even an upturned hat in your classroom. Every now and then invite parents to send in a slip of paper with an 'opening line' written on it. Ensure that the container is always full. Every week have a session in which the class pass around the hat and pull out a story opener. The child then writes a story using the opening line that they receive.

In the past, I have asked parents to write their name next to the opening line and then children can pass the story on to the person who submitted the opening line. Or I have posted the stories online on the school website or blog. This is a nice way to keep parents involved by having them participate in writing activities in the classroom and enabling them to see what was created through their input.

Another method which I have found successful is for children to select a book either from the book corner in the classroom or the school library. They open to the first page and read the opening line. They then write their own story using that same line.

Story mash-up

The idea behind this writing activity is that children select characters from a variety of books, movies or TV shows and blend them together to create their own stories. This is a really easy way to grab children's attention and works especially well as a free-writing exercise as children have a clear starting point. There are many different ways to approach this. I usually start by asking children to select one of their favourite characters and then to choose a setting from a different TV show or book. They then combine these two elements together and write about the results. It does not have to be a full-blown story, but the result allows children to really engage and unleash their imaginations in a way that gives them free rein over characters and settings that they're already invested in and love.

Comic books

These are always very popular with young children. I like to provide blank comic strip worksheets and allow children to complete these as they choose to do so. Another way to achieve this is to use software which allows children to create an animated story online. There are lots of different programs which have been designed to accomplish this and most schools have something on their ICT system which enables pupils to do this.

The spontaneously replenishing box

Wrap an old cardboard box in gift paper and leave it in the classroom. Tell children that it is a magic box that will refill itself with whatever they choose whenever they want it to do so. Ask them what they would choose to refill the box with and then to write about what they chose and why they chose that item. What happens when they open the box? Ask them to write about what they imagine will happen. I establish some rules: the box cannot be filled with money or anything that would hurt anybody. Give them some ideas to start with: doughnuts, pencils, a new puppy, bananas. The choices are never-ending.

Pocket pet

Imagine that you can choose any wild animal that could be shrunk down to be small enough to carry around in your pocket. What animal would you choose to be your pocket pet and why? Rhino? Alligator? Cheetah? Giraffe? What would day-to-day life be like with your new pet? What would happen when you brought it to school or to your grandmother's house or the supermarket? Describe a day with your imaginary pet.

Super songs

Create a superhero and a supervillain. Write about their traits and their strengths and weaknesses. Think about the sort of things that these characters both want. Now write a song for both of them to sing. They need one each. Imagine that your superhero likes to sing his or hers whilst driving their car. Imagine that your villain likes to sing their song whilst in-between plotting dastardly deeds. Ask your children to write the lyrics to their songs. Then allow them to perform them to each other. This usually works best when done in groups. Provide musical instruments, such as tambourines and xylophones etc, for the children to use.

The best school trip ever!

If you could plan our next school trip, where would you take us to and why? Funfair or beach? Fishing? Rollerblading? To a football match? Ask children to choose a place that they would want to take the class and then write about all the reasons why we should go there. The writing should take the form of a letter. Not only are they trying to persuade the teacher why they should take the trip because of all the fun aspects involved, but they also need to think about the sorts of things that the class could learn whilst they were on the trip. Don't forget to include things like transport and what the arrangements would be for lunch. Don't feel that you need to stick to normal sorts of trips. If you want to go on a pirate ship or to the moon that's absolutely fine.

King/Queen of the world

You have just found out that you are the King/Queen of the whole world and from now on you are in charge of absolutely everything. You have to make decisions about the laws and what people have to do. Think about some of the things that you would like to change about the world. Think about the laws that you want to put in place. These can be as serious or as silly as you like. Perhaps you want to ban all PE lessons, or maybe you want to make it a rule that every Tuesday is ice-cream day. Think about the sorts of things you would do and write about them.

Over the mountain

Imagine you got to the top of a previously unexplored mountain. Well done! You are enjoying the view and then you look over the other side and to your astonishment you see …

What do you see? Tell us all about it. And then tell us what happened when you went down to that side of the mountain.

Yuck!

Write about a food that you hate. What is it that you do not like about this food? When do you have to eat this food? Is there a reason that people want you to eat it? Do you think that there are some benefits to eating food that we don't like?

Film and book reviews

Ask children to write reviews of books that they have read at home and bring them in. Display these in the book corner and post them onto your website. Also, do the same for films. Let the children read out their reviews in class.

Think about starting a 'film club' in which parents are invited to watch a film each week with their children and then they come in and discuss the film with the children in your class for a short period each week. Encourage all the children to write reviews about the films that they have watched. At the end of the term, choose your favourite films and rank them.

Happy day

Write instructions for how to have a really happy day. Include ideas and suggestions for things to see and do as well as writing about how to behave.

Dinner with someone famous

You have been invited to have dinner with your favourite famous person. Who is this person? Why are they famous and what do they do? What is it about them that makes you like them? What foods do you eat and what sort of things do you talk about and show the person?

Redesign the school

If you could redesign the school, what would you do to make it different? Maybe you would add a swimming pool on the roof or perhaps a Ferris wheel and a fast food restaurant. What about the school uniform, what sort of colours would you use or would you even make the children wear a uniform at all?

And now for some really short writing prompts

■ What are you really good at doing? What do you wish you were better at? Do we all have to be the same?

■ Why is it important to be nice to others? Write a list of 10 things you can do to practise kindness to others.

■ What have you got in your life that makes you lucky? We take a lot for granted. Tell us what are you grateful for and why?

■ Write a letter to your grown-up self. What do you want to remember as a grown up and what do you want to make sure that you are doing in 20 years time? Remind yourself.

■ Write a letter to the author of a book you recently read and tell them what you liked most about the book.

■ What are you thinking about right at this moment?

Using Drama

Drama is a fantastic method to assist you in the development of literacy in your classroom. Speaking and listening skills are boosted through dramatic based approaches, role-play, improvisation and as a result of the discussion and contribution of thoughts and feelings that instinctively occurs in group activities. Drama can be used as a framework to improve writing skills, to write dialogue and to broaden vocabulary. Improvisation and storytelling foster children's understanding of how to construct a narrative and this consequently impacts positively on speaking and writing abilities.

I strongly advocate the use of drama as a source of ideas for writing. Drama activities are a really fun and effective way of promoting first-rate thinking and dialogue, as well as resulting in good written outcomes. There are various drama exercises which can aid in preparing children to produce written work. The exercises below facilitate preparation and planning for writing in various ways. Some of them are useful in helping to create the relationships between characters and their settings. Others help children to manage the entwining of description (setting and minor characters), action (including background action) and dialogue (or 'thoughts').

Drama exercises linked to creative writing can support children in creating and developing characters when writing fiction. They establish that characters are sometimes multifaceted and have a history, a background, views and opinions, interests, hopes and fears. Some of these activities allow children to 'meet' a character in role and to amass information about them in a drama situation before writing. Children can use the information they gather as a resource to help them create a rich and thought-provoking character when they write.

Drama can be incorporated into literacy lessons in order to extend the children's understanding of characters and situations or to imagine different outcomes. Debate through drama allows children to discuss and share ideas about a narrative as well as to summarise the main points of a story, consider character behaviour and think about how to communicate ideas.

Drama in the Foundation Stage

Drama is fundamental to Early Years settings. Taking on a role and pretending to be someone else in imagined situations and acting out stories are vital activities for the Foundation Stage. The role-play area and other play situations provide opportunities for children to experience and develop their early dramatic skills. But using structured drama games is also beneficial to strengthen both vocal and written communication.

Drama in Key Stage 1

During Key Stage 1, pupils move from make-believe dramatic play for themselves to a more deliberately planned form of drama. Engaging pupils in activities that allow them to explore their ideas is highly valuable. In participating in the following activities, children become increasingly aware of their audience. This skill benefits their writing.

When the children are deeply familiar with stories, characters and circumstances, as a result of having been engaged in the storytelling process, the writing produced is frequently of a high standard. Allowing children to physically act out and take on the voices of characters which they will then use in their writing is highly valuable. Allowing children to collaborate in such a memorable, playful and engaging way provides circumstances which motivate them as writers. In producing writing which is meaningful to them as a writer, confidence is also strengthened as well as self-belief in their writing abilities.

Countless drama techniques allow children to become immersed into the situation and setting of a character. Making use of methods – such as hot-seating, conscience alleys, debates and improvisation – engages children fully and can strengthen their understanding of a text as well as their aptitude to articulate their views in written form. These methods are discussed further below.

For instance, taking a dramatic approach to understanding how it feels to be homeless can result in a much more meaningful understanding of poverty and the experience of living on the street. In turn, this helps the children to write more contemplatively and imaginatively.

Freeze-frame

Children collaborate either in small groups or a whole class. They then 'perform' a moment that presents the action in a narrative frozen in time, as if the pause button on a DVD has been pushed. This permits them to consider what is happening with each of the characters or to contemplate what is happening from different points of view. Perhaps the actual moment in question may be the attention-grabbing point. Alternatively, they may wish to discuss what has just transpired or is about to take place. For this activity to be successful, children should have appropriate contextual information of the situation for the freeze-frame, to appreciate their own character in the action, or as an audience member, to be able to discuss it.

Thinking aloud

After the freeze-frame has been fashioned, the teacher should move between the characters in the scene. Pick one child at a time to take on the role of the character they are playing and vocalise their thoughts. This allows all the children in the audience to understand what all of the characters are thinking at that very moment in time. It gives hints about the role each child is playing and is a really good way to discuss different viewpoints in narratives.

Slow mo

Choose a character in the freeze-frame. That child should repeat the action that they previously performed. This time, however, they do it in an exaggerated slow way, as though they are moving in slow motion. This allows the audience to contemplate not only the action that is occurring, but the reason for why it is taking place. Alternatively, another child can narrate the slow-motion action that is taking place. You can then scribe this onto a whiteboard. This is a useful way to look at different ways to present action in fiction. I like to look at passive and active verbs when doing this exercise. This is especially useful for Year 2 and above.

Thought tracking

This is similar to the *Thinking aloud* activity because it enables the class to track one particular character's train of thought through the action taking place. In this exercise, ask several children to act out the freeze-frame in slow motion whilst they vocalise their thoughts. This is an excellent way for the characters to reveal their feelings, motivations and viewpoints. After doing this drama exercise with a class, I like the children to write a scene from several different character's points of view. I usually stick to three or four characters in a scene and allow the children to choose who they would like to write about. Sometimes I use characters whom the children are familiar with from popular TV shows; sometimes we create the characters from scratch.

The drama activities below allow children to rehearse two different sides of an argument or explore different viewpoints and are useful preparation for discursive writing and persuasion texts.

'Conscience alley' or 'thought tunnel'

This exercise is a way of exploring the thoughts of characters. It provides children with a chance to reflect, in detail, on the motivating factors of a character and their dilemmas at a specific moment in time, for example, should the Billy Goat cross the bridge? Should Jack chop down the beanstalk? Ask the children to form two lines and stand facing each other. Each line takes on a contrasting viewpoint. You may wish to allow children to select which side of the line they want to stand on. Or, you may decide to divide the class up yourself and choose for them.

One child is selected to stroll slowly down the 'alley' as the children on each side of the line vocalise their opinion on a topic. After completing the walk, and listening to the voices, this pupil then has to decide what their decision will be. You can allow the child to repeat the walk. Or, perhaps, you will allow more than one pupil to have a turn. This means that children can have a turn at being on either side of the argument, if you rotate the lines. The benefits of this exercise are that it can deepen a child's understanding of a character's situation and allow them to develop empathy. They are better able to consider the different viewpoints available to the character, as well as to think about their motivations and possible actions. After doing this drama exercise, ask children to go away and write two alternate paragraphs: one in which the character takes action by the first line; the second the action that would occur if they were persuaded by the alternate viewpoint advocated.

Overheard conversations

This drama activity should be used after the 'conscience alley' drama exercise. The children overhear a conversation that they would not usually have access to. They then can use this additional knowledge to reflect on its bearing on a narrative, or a state of affairs. For example, the class may have been using conscience alley to explore two different sides of an argument. Should Jack sell the cow? Yes, because they need the money. No, because the cow would be sad and they would miss her, and she may not be looked after properly.

Then introduce two or more characters who are in some way connected with the situation. The class eavesdrops on a conversation they have. For example, when the main character reaches the end of the conscience alley, the children all sit down and 'accidentally overhear' the conversation between two people who are on their way to the market. They discuss how they have always wanted a cow and would take such good care of her and give her a lovely home. The overheard conversation has to include precise communication that sways the situation. As a teacher, you will prepare the children beforehand with what to say; you can whisper in their ears if they forget. Now, ask the child who was playing Jack, and walked down the alley, what his decision is about selling the cow. He will be more likely to sell her, knowing that she will go to a good home and that he can then take some money home to his mother. Ask the children to work in groups to think of some other 'overheard' conversations that might impact Jack's decision. Then ask the children to write these different scenarios up.

Collective voice

Ask the class to gather round in a circle. For this exercise, you as the teacher will take on the role of one speaker in a conversation. The entire class takes on the part of a single, second speaker. As the teacher, you will start the conversation, talking to the 'other person' (the class). Any child can speak to continue the dialogue, ask them to raise their hand, and you will indicate who can talk. (Otherwise it just gets confusing, with lots of talking over each other.) Inform the class that they have a common purpose to try to find out some specific information or for them to give advice. Children usually manage the 'communal role' well because they are focused on what the first character (the teacher) has to say and they want to find out more. Once children are familiar with this activity, the class can take on the more responsible role of the character with information to pass on. I have used this in lots of different ways. For instance, asking the children to try to find out where we are going on a class trip that term. Or, if we are playing characters, asking 'bad guys' to reveal their crimes. For instance, in a superhero topic, this activity works well if the teacher pretends to be the villain and the class are the superhero. The class need to find out where the villain has hidden the kidnapped person, super-weapon or stolen gold. The potential is endless. As always, this activity leads on nicely to linked writing activities.

Using art displays

It's worth mentioning that it's possible to inspire and motivate children to write using art displays which they have contributed to as a prompt. I frequently use not only board displays, but also 3D displays which I create inside and outside. Here is an example of a Halloween garden display which I created with my class. I set it up, as a surprise for the children to see on their way to school as they passed the school gate. They had helped to make the Jack o' lanterns. I added the other items. When they arrived at school, excited about the scene they had seen, they wrote stories about the 'Broomstick Ball'.

Bringing it all Together

The methods which I have outlined in this book work and will deliver strong results. There isn't a set format to follow; rather it is up to you as a teacher to plan how to incorporate the suggestions and ideas into your own practice and school and ascertain how to make them work in your own classroom. As you are designing your curriculum think about the different topics which you are going to be covering and how these lend themselves to the areas which I have outlined.

I cannot stress enough how much I recommend using a variety of these exercises and methods throughout the school year. It is through doing a combination of these things that I have been able to assist children to reach their full potential as writers, achieve strong academic results and to have a love of writing.

To recap:

1. I wholeheartedly recommend spending 5 to 10 minutes a day calling out the digraphs which are appropriate to your particular year group, until the children can recall these independently and without the need to refer to sound cards. I usually do this for the whole year. Even once the sounds have taken root in a child's short term memory, it is common for the information not to become fully embedded. Therefore, it is worth the few minutes a day that it takes to really give children a secure and deep-rooted knowledge of these building blocks of words. Also, incorporate a few tricky words a week into this activity and children will rapidly build up the ability to spell these non-phonetic words off by heart as well as learning spelling rules which they can then apply to word families. Remember to also offer a variety of other appropriate phonic activities which are appropriate to your class's needs and that practise reading, writing, segmenting and blending skills.

2. Introduce a 'Picture of the day' activity and use it in a variety of ways. Always ask children to consider *Who? What? Why? Where?* and *When?* whilst discussing the picture. And don't forget about *How?* As the school year progresses, ask children to incorporate ideas that you have taught them about character development, setting, show, don't tell and the other creative writing tools which they're starting to get under their belts. Ask the children to create free-writing exercises linked to the picture or to tell oral stories. These sessions only have to last 10 minutes or so, or can last for a whole English session.

   I have used this exercise in many ways. An example (on page 132) shows some writing which my class did after I printed out a picture and left it taped to a whiteboard. All the writing was independent. Children wandered up to jot ideas down throughout the day.

   You may decide to link pictures to the topic of the term. For example, for a *Castles* topic, you might look at a picture of knights jousting (page 133).

3. Allow the children to have a session each day in which they're free to simply draw a picture and write about it. Give them total autonomy about what they write.

4. Set homework. It does not have to be a huge task, but weekly spellings and daily reading make a massive contribution to children's progress.

5. Encourage children to complete writing at home and celebrate it with a daily 'show and tell' session.

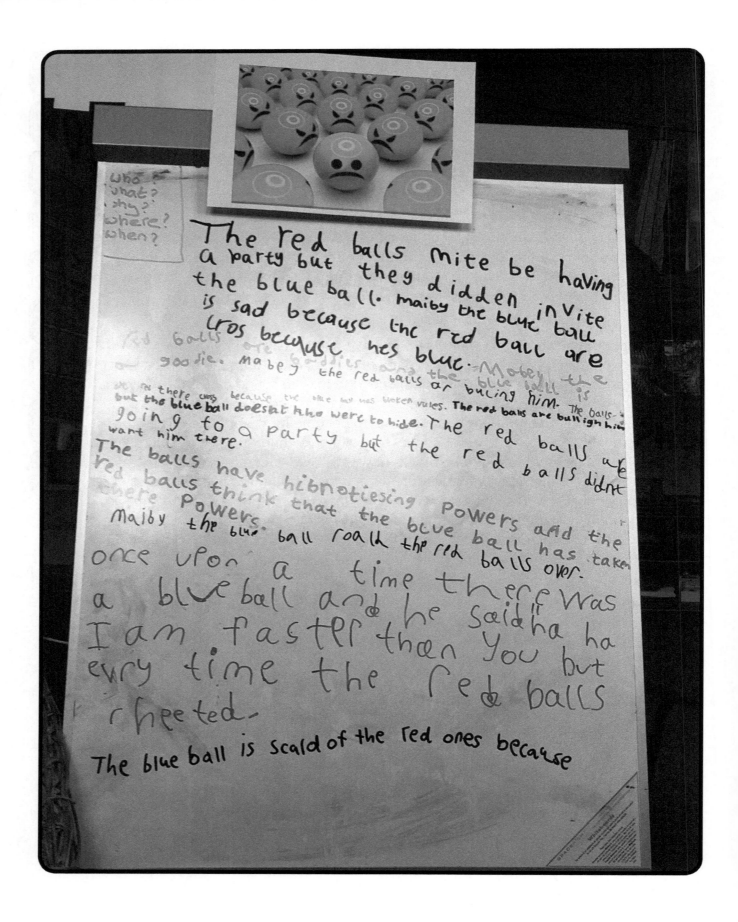

who?
what?
why?
where?
when?

The red balls mite be having a party but they didden invite the blue ball. maiby the blue ball is sad because the red ball are cros becuase hes blue. Mabey the red balls are goodies and the blue ball is a goodie. mabey the red balls ar buling him. the balls are ther cros because the blue ball has broken rules. The red balls are bulligh him but the blue ball doesnt kho were to hide. The red balls are going to a party but the red balls didnt want him there.

The balls have hibnotiesing Powers and the red balls think that the blue ball has taken there powers. maiby the blue ball roald the red balls over.

once upon a time there was a blue ball and he saidha ha I am faster than you but evry time the red balls r rheeted.

The blue ball is scald of the red ones because

How to Achieve Outstanding Writers in the Early Years Foundation Stage and Key Stage 1

6. When the children are writing at their tables, I recommend having music playing in the background. I like to use jazz. Sometimes, however, I link it to the current topic, for instance, on the occasion when my class were taking part in the castle topic, I played medieval music. I find that setting a mood can really inspire children.

7. Whatever is going on in the school calendar, I have always made it an absolute rule to never ever drop my phonics sessions or writing sessions. It can be easy to miss a session here and there, and before you know it, the time really adds up. Frequent and consistent is key.

8. Bring in weekly 'creative exercises' linked to teaching creative writing as a skill. These really are a key part of becoming a strong writer when creating stories. It simply isn't taught to young children, yet they're able to grasp the concepts.

All of these things combined together enable children to write stories based on photographs, pictures or props. Ideally, all these things (goals, internal struggles, external struggles, strengths, and weaknesses) will tie in with a central plot and become woven together through the story's subplots and themes. Children will begin to combine these concepts naturally when they're writing. Of course, they will realise that there is no requirement to include it all.

Teaching children these methods produces motivated and capable writers who are far beyond their years academically. Children will reap the benefits of this in so many ways.

Writing is an essential life skill. It is incredibly important that young children learn the underpinnings of writing at a young age, so they're not behind when these writing skills matter. The better they are at writing, the stronger start they have in their academic lives. Clear writing is an indication of understanding and clarity of thoughts. Good writers know how to articulate themselves, they make things easy to understand and they know when to leave out the unnecessary. Children will grasp how to express themselves well and to communicate ideas.

In the age of emojis, writing helps children to be able to express themselves bettre both orally and in written form. This means that they are therefore able to communicate ideas more effectively. Mobile phones and tablets are an everyday part of life now, and 'text speak' and 'smiley faces' are part of everyday language. It's now more important than ever that children are assisted in building their vocabulary and in becoming eloquent at expressing themselves. In this age of social media and instant messaging, texts and emails, our vocabulary is frequently changing. In fact, some even consider that the emoji is the swiftest growing 'language' in the world. Children are growing up in a world where the use of the emoji in many circumstances is more conventional than the use of actual grammar. It isn't an exaggeration to consider that the impact of this can be detrimental to literacy and could have a damaging impact on real-world communication.

Regular writing has been demonstrated to be a highly effective means of assisting children to improve their communication skills. So ensuring time in the classroom to enable them to write on a regular basis will assist in reducing any fear of them not being exposed to ways in which they gain the ability to communicate effectively.

Writing helps children to attain better results in STEM subjects such as science and maths. Many studies have been carried out which have concluded that writing helps the brain to acquire the analytical functions which assist in acquiring an aptitude for maths and science.

Creative writing helps children to process stress and trauma. By introducing creative writing into children's lives, they can be taught to process stressful or traumatic events in a healthy way while recovering from these events faster and learning how to become more resilient. Following on from classroom or playground incidents, I often ask children to write a recount and then discuss this from the other person's point of view. This helps to develop empathy and the ability to reflect upon their own behaviour. Creative writing has also been shown to reduce stress levels.

Writing improves reading ability. Writing and reading go together naturally. When children create text and increase the quantity of writing they do, this then results in an increase in reading comprehension, as well as improved writing skills.

With all of these advantages, it is evident that creative writing can have an incredibly positive impact on a child's development in many different ways.

I hope that you have found this book useful and that you are able to use it to assist you in passing on these benefits to the children in your own classrooms.

Index

Photo-credits

Every effort has been made to trace copyright holders and to obtain their permissions. The publisher apologises for any omissions in the list above and would be grateful for notification of any corrections that should be incorporated in future reprints or editions of this book.

P.12 Colouring; Cindy Parks: Pixabay

P.22 Little girl; Trevor M: Pixabay

P.25 Kids; Klimkin: Pixabay

P.30 Hans Christian Andersen; Ronile: Pixabay

P.31 Jack and the beanstalk illustration; Gaynor Barrs

P.35 Peter Pan illustration; Gaynor Barrs

P.38 Man Texting; Clem Onojeghuo: Stocksnap

P.39 The Magician; Vasili: Pixabay

P.40 Cat Grass; Pasja 1000: Pixabay

P.41 Asian Boy Lantern; Sasin Tipchai: Pixabay

P.42 Hotair Balloon; StockSnap_2SFV3ZUNWZ

P.45 Beach; Public Domain Pictures: Pixabay

P.46 Lightning; Adrian Lang: Pixabay

P.48 Dentist; Michal Jarmoluk: Stocksnap

P.51 Wooden Horse; Skeeze: Pixabay

P.52 Hong Kong at night; Garyrabbit: Absfreepic

P.53 Tee-pee; Erika Wittlieb: Pixabay

P.53 Badger; Vincent-van-Zalinge: Upsplash

P.57 Message; Marvington: Pixabay

P.58 The bike in a tree in 2006; KendianaJones (May 2015) Vashon Island: Tripadvisor

P.59 Person-tree By Blackash at English Wikipedia, CC BY 3.0, https://commons.wikimedia.org/w/index.php?curid=52493598

P.60 Girl; Pezibear: Pixabay

P.61 Cowboys; Skeeze: Pixabay

P.62 Skateboard; Freephotos; Pixabay

P.63 Architecture; Stockphoto: Stocksnap

P.64 Giraffes; Christine Spoonchia: Pixabay

P.65 Hand-in-hand; Andy: Absfreepic

P.66 Machu Picchu; Logga Wiggler: Pixabay

P.67 Train; David Mark: Pixabay

P.68 Yacht; vladimirya: Pixabay

P.69 Sunflower; Stephen Walker: Unsplash

P.70 Feet; Candice McDaniel: Stocksnap
Police; Andrew Martin: Pixabay

P.73 People/surfing; Stocksnap: Pixabay

P.74 Microphone; FreePhotos: Pixabay

P.75 Robot; Fernando Zhiminaicela: Pixabay

P.76 Blur; Pexels: Pixabay

P.77 Children; Wilkie Images: Pixabay

P.78 Stay-at-home; Souman82hazra: Pixabay

P.79 Beggar; Tom Parsons: Unsplash

P.81 Blue-eyed boy: ABSfreepic.com

P.82 Angry Man; Ashish Choudary: Pixabay

P.83 Water Skiing; David Mark: Pixabay

P.85 Talladega; David Mark: Pixabay

P.86 Hiding; Free Photos: Pixabay

P.89 Men; 5688709: Pixabay

P.90 Hands/ candle; Myriam Zilles: Pixabay

P.101 Dew; Frank Lisbman: Pixaby

P.102 Cheese; Nicole Pankalla: Pixabay

P.103 New York; Robert Jones: Pixabay

P.104 Elephant; MstfKckVG: Pixabay

P.105 Bananas; Pixel 2013: Pixabay

P.106 Castle; MW: Pixabay

P.108 Knowledge; Gerdx Altmann: Pixabay

P.112 Child's game; Stocksnap

P.116 Talking cat; Javardh: Upsplash

P.130 Halloween; Rowena Woods

P.132 Red balls; Rowena Woods

P.133 Joust; Clarence Alford: Pixabay

Photo-credits for PowerPoint Slides

Every effort has been made to trace copyright holders and to obtain their permissions. The publisher apologises for any omissions in the list above and would be grateful for notification of any corrections that should be incorporated in future reprints or editions of this book.

Story Starters
Little Girl; Trevor M: Pixabay
Hans Christian Andersen; Ronile: Pixabay

Teaching about Character
Man Texting; Clem Onojeghuo: Stocksnap
The Magician; Vasili: Pixabay
Cat Grass; Pasja 1000: Pixabay
Asian Boy Lantern; Sasin Tipchai: Pixabay
Sailboat; Jaquekine Macou: Pixabay

Teaching about Setting
Hotair Balloon; StockSnap_2SFV3ZUNWZ
Beach; Public Domain Pictures: Pixabay
Lightning; Adrian Lang: Pixabay
Wooden Horse; Skeeze: Pixabay
Hong Kong at night; Garyrabbit: Absfreepic
Tee-pee; Erika Wittlieb: Pixabay
Badger; Vincent-van-Zalinge: Upsplash
Hanging clock, Antiques House: ABSfreepic.com
Train; David Mark: Pixabay
Gugus-gugus_5Eolaz8fckc-unsplash
Background; jplenio: Pixabay

Plot: Narrative Hooks
Puzzle hook
   Message; Marvington: Pixabay
   The bike in a tree in 2006; KendianaJones
     (May 2015) Vashon Island: Tripadvisor
   Person-tree by Blackash at English:
     Wikipedia, CC BY 3.0, https://commons.
     wikimedia.org/w/index.php?crid=52493598
Action hook
   Human; Pezibear: Pixabay
   Cowboys; Skeeze: Pixabay
   Horse racing; hhash: Pixabay
   Skateboard; Freephotos; Pixabay
Conversation/dialogue hook
   Architecture; Stockphoto: Stocksnap
   Giraffes; Christine Spoonchia: Pixabay
   Hand-in-hand; Andy: Absfreepic
   Asian children; Syaibatul Hamdi: Pixabay

Scenic/Setting description hook
   Machu Picchu; Logga Wiggler: Pixabay
   Train; David Mark: Pixabay
   Yacht; Vladimirya: Pixabay
Character hook
   Sunflower; Stephen Walker: Unsplash
   Feet; Candace McDaniel: StockSnap
   Policeman; Dean Moriarty: Pixabay
   Fishing; Free Photos: Pixabay

Narrative Point of View
People surfing; Stocksnap: Pixabay
Microphone; Free Photos: Pixabay
Robot_FernandoZhiminaicela.Pixabay
Children; StartupStockPhotos: Pixabay
Rollercoaster Fun; Peter Linforth: Pixabay

Show, don't tell
Blur; Pexels: Pixabay
Children; Wilkie Images; Pixabay
Cat and dog cuddles;
Stay-at-home; Souman82hazra: Pixabay
Beggar; Tom Parsons: Unsplash
Blue-eyed boy: ABSfreepic.com
Angry Man; Ashish Choudary: Pixabay
Cuddles; Stocksnap
Beggar; Dean Moriarty:Pixabay
Boathouse; Frank Winkler: Pixabay
CryingEyes; QuaimSadiq: StockSnap

Action and Dialogue
Water Skiing; David Mark: Pixabay
Talladega; David Mark: Pixabay
Hiding; Free Photos: Pixabay
Men; 5688709: Pixabay
Boxing; Wilkie Images: Pixabay
Rollercoaster; Ethan Hoover: Unsplash
Metro bus; F. Muhammed: Pixabay

Poetry

<u>5-line Sensory Poems</u>
Dew; Frank Lisbman: Pixaby
Cheese; Nicole Pankalla: Pixabay
New York; Robert Jones: Pixabay
Grundarfjorur; MustangJoe:Pixabay
Fairy Lights?; Matthew Bartelli:Stocksnap
Times Square; Serinfgar: Pixabay

<u>7-line Sensory Poems</u>
Fair ground; Ethan Hoover: Unsplash
Rollercoaster; paologhedini: Pixabay
Apple Pie; Bjurvoll Hansen: Pixabay
BlowingBubbles; Jesline: Pixabay

<u>Nonsense Poetry</u>
Eletelephony
Bananas; Pixel 2013: Pixabay
Castle; MW: Pixabay
Weather-vane; Holger Schué: Pixabay

Non-fiction Writing

Knowledge; Gerd Altmann: Pixabay
Board game : Stocksnap
Javardh; AHEpAdR8Xo: Unsplash
Teddy; Kurt K:Pixabay
Pumkin Garden Rowena Woods

Picture of the Day

Free-Writing; Rowena Woods
La-boqueria; Sofia Daranyi: Pixabay
Talking dog; Bryan Debin: Unsplash
Ceiba-speciosa; BabaMüller: Pixabay
Fish; ChristelSagniez: Pixabay

Lightning Source UK Ltd.
Milton Keynes UK
UKHW051119101121
393631UK00008B/50